PRACTICAL CHRISTIANITY

*Essays on
The Practice of Religion*

BY
RUFUS M. JONES, A. M., Litt. D.
PROFESSOR OF PHILOSOPHY IN HAVERFORD COLLEGE

New and Enlarged Edition

Wipf & Stock
PUBLISHERS
Eugene, Oregon

Wipf and Stock Publishers
199 W 8th Ave, Suite 3
Eugene, OR 97401

Practical Christianity
Essays on the Practice of Religion
By Jones, Rufus M.
ISBN: 1-59752-643-6
Publication date 4/14/2006
Previously published by The John C. Winston Co., 1905

Dedication

TO THE STUDENTS OF HAVERFORD COLLEGE WITH WHOM
IT HAS BEEN MY PLEASURE TO SEARCH FOR TRUTH
THIS BOOK IS INSCRIBED

CONTENTS

CHAPTER		PAGE
I.	THE SUPREME DEMONSTRATION	17
II.	THINGS WHICH CANNOT BE SHAKEN	21
III.	THE GOOD FIGHT OF FAITH	24
IV.	THE TEST OF A CHURCH	27
V.	THE MAN WITHIN THE MAN	30
VI.	WRESTLING FOR THE BLESSING	33
VII.	THE MORE EXCELLENT WAY	36
VIII.	THE GIFT OF LISTENING TO GOD	39
IX.	THE MISSION OF THE CHURCH	43
X.	COMING TO GOD—THE ATONEMENT AS A PRACTICAL TRUTH	47
XI.	HEART, SOUL, STRENGTH, MIND	51
XII.	A POSTPONED HEAVEN	54
XIII.	WROUGHT FOR THE SELF-SAME THING	57
XIV.	NO SIGN SHALL BE GIVEN	60
XV.	PISGAH VIEWS OF LIFE	65
XVI.	THE VINE-STOCK	68
XVII.	THE PLACE OF THE HOME IN CIVILIZATION	71
XVIII.	THE ETERNAL NATURE OF THINGS	74
XIX.	DIVERSIONS AND RECREATIONS	77

CONTENTS

CHAPTER		PAGE
XX.	A Religion of Power	80
XXI.	Pentecost in our Christianity	83
XXII.	Worshiping God	86
XXIII.	Christians in the World	89
XXIV.	If Christ Came to the Home	92
XXV.	Christianity and Reform Work	95
XXVI.	Our Thought of God	99
XXVII.	The Father and the Son	102
XXVIII.	Beatitudes in the Gospel	106
XXIX.	What Would We Ask Him?	109
XXX.	Robes of Righteousness	112
XXXI.	Two Typical Conceptions of Salvation	115
XXXII.	Putting Off and Putting On	118
XXXIII.	To Whom Shall We Go?	121
XXXIV.	The Rarest Human Quality	124
XXXV.	Not Cunningly Devised Fables	127
XXXVI.	Sabbath Observance	130
XXXVII.	The Gospel of the Son of God	133
XXXVIII.	A Faith That Honors God	136
XXXIX.	What Might Have Been, But is Not	139
XL.	The Peace of God	142
XLI.	Is True Religion Emotional?	145
XLII.	The Downward Pressure	149
XLIII.	Does God Really Love Us?	152
XLIV.	The Incarnation	155
XLV.	A Religion of Four Anchors	158

CONTENTS

CHAPTER		PAGE
XLVI.	PRACTICAL HOLINESS	162
XLVII.	APPLIED CHRISTIANITY AND WHAT IT SEEKS	165
XLVIII.	CHRISTIAN HOLINESS	168
XLIX.	THE FOUNDING OF THE CHURCH	172
L.	THE GOSPEL OF THE KINGDOM	179
LI.	THE TEST OF CHRISTIANITY	184
LII.	THE MESSAGE OF QUAKERISM	188
LIII.	THE EFFECT OF DISCOURAGEMENT	203
LIV.	LEARNING TO LIVE IN A NEW WORLD	207
LV.	BEHIND THE GATE	211
LVI.	SOME STRANGE TRIUMPHAL CHARIOTS	214
LVII.	THE MINISTRY OF ORDINARY PEOPLE	218
LVIII.	IT WORKS	220
LIX.	UNDER THE JUNIPER TREE	223
LX.	BECOMING LIKE LITTLE CHILDREN	226
LXI.	THE MOST SERIOUS SCEPTICISM	230
LXII.	WHAT NOT TO PRAY FOR	233
LXIII.	THE PRACTICE OF THE LOVE OF GOD	237
LXIV.	HAS CHRISTIANITY BEEN TRIED?	241
LXV.	BEAUTY IN RELIGION	244
LXVI.	THE LIFE OF LIBERTY	247

PREFACE TO THE SECOND EDITION.

A LITTLE book, called "Brother Lawrence," has made many in our generation familiar with the phrase—"practising the presence of God." That word which meant so much to "Brother Lawrence" expresses the real aim of this book. It is written to emphasize the importance of "practising the presence of God." Volumes abound which elaborate in scholarly fashion the historical development of Christianity and which analyze the central conceptions of Christ's religion. I am pointing out in these short chapters that the best way to find out what this religion is, is to try it— *to practise it*.

It is a satisfaction to know that the world cares to have such a book; for that is what the demand for a second edition seems to mean. I have taken this opportunity to add considerable new material to the original book, and these fresh chapters, I believe, carry the main idea of the first edition farther and deeper.

The real test of the value of the book must be looked for in its practical fruits. It is written

INTRODUCTION

not to develop or defend a theory, but to attract persons to a type of life—to set men actually to practising the presence of God. It is written in the simple faith that there are many in all walks of life who are dissatisfied with forms and schemes and who are ready to answer a plain call to learn of the doctrine by *doing the will of God.*

Haverford, Pennsylvania, Autumn, 1905.

INTRODUCTION

WE do not mean to imply in the title of this book that there are two kinds of Christianity,—one kind which is "practical" and one that is not. We simply mean that this book does not deal with speculative problems, but with the facts of life.

It is said of Socrates that he brought philosophy down out of the heavens to the earth. The statement means that Socrates abandoned the fruitless speculations of the early Greek philosophers concerning the origin of the universe and the constitution of the heavens and the earth, and sought instead for a practical method of life. How can a man realize in his own life the highest Good? *This* is the all important question with him.

In a much truer sense Jesus Christ brought religion out of the heavens to the earth. He does not speculate, He does not theorize, He announces and illustrates and exemplifies a way and method of life. Religion and life with Him mean the same thing.

We have since put His teaching, with that of His immediate followers, into a system which we call Christian theology, but the moment we go back to the primitive facts of Christianity, we find not a cold and rigid system of thought and belief, but a Life, a message, a Personality—a manifestation of God and a revelation of the true meaning of humanity. In Him we have a Son of God and a Son of man living among men to show life on its true scale.

There is nothing in His message which does not bear directly upon our human life. He took not the nature of angels, He talked not of the angelic, the seraphic, the celestial realm, He admitted us into none of the secrets of a foreign world; He took the nature of men, He showed how a man might become a son of God and He unfolded the method and laws of the kingdom of heaven—the ideal social order in which men shall be sons of God and brothers one to the other.

INTRODUCTION

Christianity is not Christianity until it is *applied* to life. It cannot be reduced to a bloodless theory, an abstract scheme any more than a pressed flower can be a genuine violet. It must not stop short of its purpose, which is, as a vital force, to reconstruct man and society and to work out as a fact the spirit of Jesus Christ in the individual, and in the social organism. One may almost take as Christ's final message his own great words, "*Know* the Truth" and "*Do* the Truth." The two go together, and together they complete the circuit, for the truth can never be completely known except through a *practice |of it* in the process of life.

It is a characteristic of our age to care only for that which can be applied to some use. We have slight taste for the abstract. But it is also true that our age is concerned for the expansion of the individual life and for the regeneration of society. Now it is precisely here that the Gospel of Jesus Christ meets our need and fits our condition. His purpose is to give abundant life and to make all things new and we find His message *constructive* at every point. It simply needs to be applied as we are applying the other forces which are progressively being discovered for our uses.

This book is not a systematic treatise or exposition of Practical Christianity; it is rather a series of short essays, which illustrate and interpret phases of the Practical Christian life, which indicate the method of the kingdom and which seek to manifest the Spirit's power in the life and society of our time. Most of these chapters have already been printed as editorials, but it is hoped that they may have a further service in this collected form. Chapter LII, on the Message of Quakerism is now printed for the first time. It is not intended to be a complete interpretation of Quakerism, nor is the point of view here set forth confined to Quakersism by any means. It is merely an attitude of life and teaching which has been characteristic of Friends and which for want of a better title is here called the Message of *Quakerism*.

> "Forgive them where they fail in truth
> And in thy wisdom make me wise."

Haverford, Pennsylvania, 1899.

CHAPTER I

THE SUPREME DEMONSTRATION

CHRISTIANS are continually being asked to prove that Christianity is true, and they generally point to the various books of "evidences" as an answer. There are historical proofs, monumental proofs, literary proofs, so that the events of the life of Jesus are as well authenticated as any events of antiquity. But we are told that Christianity makes assumptions of a Divine origin and a Divine manifestation which no amount of historical evidence could ever prove after nineteen hundred years. It claims an Incarnation, and it assumes that through Christ God gives men eternal life. How can any book of evidence prove such claims as that? Must we not admit that no proof is possible? The two leading exponents of apostolic Christianity—Paul and John—have given us a method of proof or demonstration which is peculiarly suited to the temper and spirit of our modern ways of thinking and of testing truth. John says, "He that believeth on the Son of God hath the witness in himself," and Paul, on the top wave of his great inspiration, says, "The Spirit itself beareth witness with our spirit, that we are the children of God." In other words the supreme demonstration of spiritual truths is an internal evidence—a witness within the soul itself. We know by immediate, first-hand knowledge that two and two are four, or that the shortest distance between two points is a straight line, or that a thing cannot both be and not be at the same time. These things are self-evident, we say. The mind is of such a nature that we cannot doubt them. In the same way we "prove" our own existence—we have the witness within ourselves, and no amount of argument could ever shake us out of the conviction, for it is based on first-hand evidence. Now our two apostles bring the whole content of spiritual revelation—the mighty message of eternal life—down to a test of a similar demonstration. It is not dependent upon historical evidence alone; it is open to the same proof as our axioms of mathematics, or even our own existence.

Christianity professes to be a revelation from God; it proclaims salvation from sin, and a new life in Christ; it offers the privilege of sonship with God, and it promises to fill believers with the spirit of love. Now the only possible proof of such claims and promises is the demonstration of personal experience. "Try it and see," is all we can say to the skeptical. It would be impossible to prove that two and two are four to a person who had no internal faculty of perceiving mathematical truth; it would, too, be impossible to prove to a man that he existed if he had no self-consciousness of it. So, too, the only proof that we have power through Christ "to become sons of God," IS TO BECOME ONE; the only demonstration that He can save from sin and give new life is TO BECOME SAVED AND TO RECEIVE THE NEW LIFE. Does anybody want any better evidence of the greatest spiritual truths of Christianity? The only evidence of the sunrise is that you see it with your own eyes; the only evidence that one's mother is good and loving is that one FEELS her love.

Thus in our last resort we fall back upon the "demonstration of the Spirit," and cry back with this witness within, "Abba, Father." We know Christ is Divine, for He has worked a divine work within *us;* we know He has power over sin, for He has taken away *ours;* we know that He brings spiritual life, for He has quickened us, and made us sit in heavenly places; we know that the atonement is a reality, for we have been reconciled with God, and are at peace with Him. Scholastic theology dealt with abstractions, and based its doctrines on logic and authority; apostolic Christianity bases itself on the demonstration of the Spirit of God to the spirit of man, on the witness within, the supreme evidence—the soul's grasp of first-hand truth. The revival of this apostolic position characterizes primitive Quakerism.

CHAPTER II

THINGS WHICH CANNOT BE SHAKEN

IN this world of ours all our spiritual truths, all our eternal realities, have to be *expressed* in temporal, human and changing forms. No matter how pure and exalted the truths, its embodiment must be more or less imperfect. In fact, it is absolutely impossible to find a permanent and unvarying expression for any idea. There have been stagnant centuries which have kept unchanged the crystallized forms which they inherited, and they have supposed that faith would cease to be if this particular form of truth should vanish away. The Pharisee could not imagine a true religion without circumcision and the blood of bulls and goats; the Roman Catholic of the fifteenth century could not believe that real religion would survive if the doctrine of trans-substantiation—the real presence in the bread and wine—should be given up. The Calvinist supposed that his articles of faith were a permanent embodiment of truth and his plan of salvation the only possible one.

They all conceived of truth as something which could be expressed once for all in a form which all coming ages must keep unchanged. As well might we expect to bottle up the daylight to preserve it, or fix this infinite life about us in nature into one unchanging form, to be preserved through all seasons, years and centuries. The moment one tries to "fix" life and crystallize into a set shape, it ceases to be *life*. The characteristic of life is its power to make its own form and expression, ever changing, ever developing, ever modifying its form, and yet keeping its essence. Truth is never some dead thing which can be "laid out;" it is living, moving, quickening, outgrowing its old forms, taking on new expressions and preserving itself, as life does, by endless variations and by infinite embodiments.

There are transitions going on in every age. The things that can be shaken are removed, and the things that have waxed old vanish away. These things always bring trial to faith, for it is difficult for most persons to distinguish between the temporary form— i. e., the human embodiment—and the eternal and abiding truth which lives on in the midst of change and vanishing forms.

Here comes the great test of spiritual power and insight. Those who have "short vision" and a traditional faith build on the temporal, and cling to the form which has grown familiar and dear to them, but if anything shakes *this* their faith is shattered, and they suffer shipwreck. Those, however, who have real spiritual vision look through the temporal and fleeting, through the transitory forms and embodiments, and settle their hearts and their faith upon the eternal reality,—the Infinite Self who abides and works through all changes. Their faith blooms in the midst of transition periods; they look calmly on while "the things that can be shaken" are being removed, and they have no fear when the things which have "waxed old" are vanishing away, for they know that those things which cannot be shaken must remain. There is no safety in this present time of transition and of changing form and expression to be found by closing the eyes or hiding the head in the sand, as the ostrich is said to do. The only safe and sure course is to reach *through* the outward and find the eternal, to rest back upon the everlasting arms, to have a personal *initiation* into the riches of the glory of this "mystery" "which is Christ in you, the hope of glory," to get free in the living truth. The things which we see are temporal, the things which the spiritual vision finds real are eternal,

CHAPTER III

THE GOOD FIGHT OF FAITH

AN old man—"Paul the aged,"—who was "ever a fighter," is writing to a young man who is just learning what it means to be a Christian soldier in the Roman Empire in the First Century. His message has the nature of a battle call—"Fight the good fight of Faith,"—and for himself he says, "I have fought the good fight, I have kept the Faith." "The fight of Faith," what does that mean? What is this exultant cry, "I have kept the Faith?" It means, of course, that "the Faith" is not something which can be kept as one keeps a jewel or a money bag, or as one keeps a pressed flower between the leaves of a book. It is something which must be struggled for, fought for and won to the very end of life.

The easier way is to have the church decide what "the Faith" is, and to have it fixed once for all, so that there shall be no necessity for struggling for it or fighting for it. The individual has then only to take it and hold it. This course the historic church took. But it paid a tremendous price for the peace and ease. It kept the Faith as the mummy tombs kept the Egyptian wheat. Its members had no necessity to fight the good fight of Faith, and their religion became a dead, nerveless, unproductive thing, a something put on from the outside like a coat, instead of something vital, springing out of the heart and permeating the whole personality.

Paul's battle call embodies a fundamental law of the spiritual life. Settle down to a life of slippered ease, with no fight for Faith, no struggle for Truth, no course to run, no goal to press toward, no reach beyond the grasp, and the soul's religion loses its color and its sap as the pressed flower does. What is more pitiable than the Christian who has no onward life, who knows that he is a Christian only because he remembers the date of his conversion, and who has no clearer evidence than his signature to the creed of his church? Paul would certainly not call this "keeping the Faith." "Keeping the Faith" for him is always bound up with ACTION. It cannot be separated from fighting the good fight and running the course to the finish.

What should we think of a mother who should discover a method of keeping her baby always a baby—who should hold up the poor dwarfed and stunted thing and say, "See, I have kept my child!" No, the way to "keep" a child is to let it take its true life-course, to let it battle with the obstacles which beset us all in this world, and so let it win an ever-increasing power. It is a course which has its dangers. The child may tumble, it may get bruises, it must have its bitter cries and its pains; but it can be a man with a man's strength in no other way.

The whole question turns upon this point: Is Faith to be something passive or something active? Is it something done once for all or a never-ending action like breathing or heart-throbbing? Is it the medal won by a single victory and kept in a case, or is it the unconquerable spirit of the fighter who never lays down his weapons, but goes from victory to victory. Paul takes the second view. It is the throb of the heart, it is the act of the soul, it is the spirit which wrings victory after victory from the enemy—in fact, faith itself *is* the victory.

CHAPTER IV

THE TEST OF A CHURCH

SOONER or later everything in this world gets tested. The things that shoot up and spread like a green bay-tree not seldom die down and pass away as soon as the real test comes. "The survival of the fittest" is a wonderful law of life, and yet we are all very slow to recognize it. We like to see things "go" at once. Prosperity and popularity dazzle our eyes, and we forget to ask, "Is it right?" But in the end we always have to learn that God has so made this world that only the excellent is permanent, only what is eternally right abides.

The Master showed clearly that the real test of a life is not popularity, not accumulation of riches, not "success," not even professions of faith—not that we have said, "Lord, Lord,"—but it is the measure in which we do God's will and make our life count in practical service. "I was sick and ye visited me," "I was thirsty and ye gave me a drink." Visiting the fatherless and widows in their affliction and keeping spotless from the world is James's test of true religion. Everywhere in the New Testament the test is a practical one,—the tree is judged by its fruits.

Well, the test of a church must be of the same practical sort. The first question is, What is it doing to meet the world's needs? Is it carrying on Christ's work, the work He went about doing? Is it interpreting Him to the world and showing that His followers have taken up His mission? Is it casting out devils, and feeding the hungry and binding up the broken-hearted, and freeing the captive and preaching the gospel to the poor and making all classes in the community believe in the present reality of God and eternal things? Or is it quibbling over some ancient tradition, or advocating some empty ceremony, or glorying in its sacred customs, or trying to "keep the faith" by shutting eyes and mind to the real questions and issues of this present time?

There are, after all, only *two* kinds of churches, though hundreds of sects. There are the churches which are alive in the Spirit, and are doing in a more or less perfect way what Christ would be doing if He were here in person, and there are the churches of various forms which seek the living among the dead. These latter all live upon and are devoted to certain things which history or tradition has made sacred. They worship "relics" of one sort or another. They are supremely concerned about these "holy things," and they suppose that Christianity will be destroyed if any of these ancient landmarks go. They limp along on crutches and wonder what would happen if one of the crutches should be lost. They never get beyond the "garments" of the Lord, and if they lost these garments everything would be gone. They are using counters instead of the real coin. Those who compose the other class have one sole and single purpose—to find Christ, to partake of His life, and to do His will. They push by all "relics" and "garments" to get to the Person Himself. They look upon the church as the body through which Christ still reaches and touches and ministers to humanity. Its work is His work. It can be done only in His spirit and in His power. It is a practical work, as His was, and its true test is its effect upon humanity. It "keeps the faith," not by crystallizing it into a form, but by continuing and maintaining in the world, the spirit, the activities, the power, the influences, which were so completely and Divinely expressed in the life of Jesus Christ.

CHAPTER V

THE MAN WITHIN THE MAN

CREATION does not stop with the making of a perfect human body, wonderful as that is. The eye, with its delicate adjustment for vibrating to color rays; the ear, with its thousands of harp-strings stretched to beat in response to the waves of sound; the wonderful brain, reaching down through its myriad network of nerves that carry out and carry in the messages; the heart, with its intricate systems of veins and arteries for reaching every cell of the body—these are as perfect as material organs can be; and the work of material creation seems complete with the production of the human body. But, alas! that which is perfect and complete is ready to vanish away, and the body no sooner gets finished than it begins to run down and wear out and waste away. It has no future; no bud of farther hope lies within it. It is the most marvelous organism and the most perfect form in the visible creation, but it dies daily until it is reduced to the dust from which it is made.

If this body of death were the crown of creation then there would be only one word for it—failure. Make the body never so perfect, and it must still come woefully short of any worthy goal. In fact, we soon find that it is the man within the visible man that we really care for. It is not the hundred or more avoirdupois pounds of flesh that we love—not the dust wreath—but the SELF that uses this visible form and speaks to us through it.

The creation and perfection of this man within are the highest ends of life so far as we have any revelation of them. This spiritual self can have but one origin—it must be born from above. It is not a thing of decaying flesh or of disintegrating matter, nor can it come from them. It comes from God, who is its home, and its perfection must go on by a divine plan—according to the law of the spirit of life which was in Christ Jesus. Like anything else, it grows by what it feeds on. It has its hungers and its thirsts which must be satisfied with real things, not with shadows.

It is clearly evident that a spiritual self cannot be forced; it must make its own choices. Its life must be formed by its own resolves and decisions. It goes up or down as it chooses. The light shines for it, the gifts of God are all about it, the heavenly visions are granted it.

the cords of an infinite love pull at it; but it decides for itself what its response shall be, and thus it chooses what its attainment shall be. The law of its being is to go from more to more. Every time it uses the light and appropriates the gift and sees the vision and responds to the love, it expands, and increases its range and scope. Every attainment is thus a prophecy of something more beyond. It can never come to its goal as the body does—that is, to the point where it must begin to run down—for its end and perfection is nothing short of likeness to Jesus Christ and the fullness of God. Its very imperfection is its glory, for it points it ever on to something which lies before. It is never left high and dry as a finished and completed thing with no more capacity for increase. The making of the man within the man is thus a continuous creation, and the desire to attain perfection is the measure of the man.

Body may go to pieces, but this spiritual self continues to be what it has made itself by its choices and its loves. The tree that grows toward the light forms its center of gravity on that side and finally falls toward the light. The soul that choose to be a son of God may wait with perfect assurance for the time when Christ shall be seen as He is, and the likeness shall be completed.

CHAPTER VI

WRESTLING FOR THE BLESSING

HOW many of us want our blessings without the struggle! If God is our loving Father, we fondly say, then he will surely give us what we need for our spiritual development without any strenuous exertion on our part. Hold up the cup, as the lily does for the dew, and it will be graciously filled. But no one can fail to find in the experiences of great spiritual souls something quite different from this—even the Captain of our salvation is made perfect through suffering and struggle. No, the spiritual stature does not come with folded hands and calm content and peaceful ease. When Jacob is to be transformed to Israel, the prince—when he is to rise to a new spiritual self—he finds that the divine form which confronts him in the dark will give no blessing until he wrestles for it.

Two of the Master's great parables embody the truth that God gives his blessings to those who show persistence and even importunity in making their desires known. Not that

God must be teased as weak human parents often are before they grant favors to their children, but it is surely best for us, for our spiritual development that all the virility and force and earnestness of our nature should go into our prayers for spiritual blessings, and that we should ask as though we *meant* to receive. There was once a poor heathen woman who met Jesus, the only time He ever crossed over the border of the little country which He called His earthly fatherland, and her heart was heavy with trouble. She had faith enough to come to this traveling Teacher, and to ask Him to cure her daughter. She poured out her request as a mother can. "And He answered her not a word." There was no sign of any help from Him. But here was a woman who would not go away without a blessing, though it might consist only of crumbs. She got not only her heart's desire, but also the beautiful words: "O woman, great is thy faith, be it unto thee as thou wishest."

It is, we believe, a mistake to suppose that the heart worships best when it is passive. The highest worship is reached when the soul *goes out actively* to wrestle with God in silence, it may be, in groanings that cannot be uttered, or in loud cryings for a truer, noblier, worthier, holier self, for the higher spiritual stature. This is what Gladstone once called " the holy *work* of worship."

God cannot be worshipped idly, sluggishly, lazily, and we need to realize that the great reason for failure in spiritual development comes from the lack of earnest, valiant wrestling for the highest good our soul can see.

CHAPTER VII

THE MORE EXCELLENT WAY

THERE is a great passage in Paul's first Corinthian letter in which he sets forth the various gifts that have been conferred upon individuals by the head of the Church for the perfecting of believers and the upbuilding of the whole body. But after unrolling the long list of lesser gifts and greater gifts and their interrelation, he suddenly sees, with his heavenly vision, the supreme thing which makes a man a son of God, and which makes a church the bride of Christ, and without which best gifts are unavailing, and he bursts forth with the words, "but I will show you a more excellent way." We all know, or should know, His more excellent way. It is better than tongues of men and of angels, it is greater than gifts of prophecy and all knowledge of mysteries, it surpasses even faith that could remove mountains, it outreaches the philanthrophy that gives and sacrifices. It is the perfect which comes when the things that are " in part " are done away. It is the face to face life with God when the dark mirror, which gives only distorted reflections, has been given up. It is the completed thing which comes after the childish things have been put away. It is the last, best, highest, divinest, heavenliest fruit the soul ever wins and that toward which the whole Divine purpose moves —love. "Follow after love," he says, and the other apostle of love says that this is the test of sonship—"he that loveth is born of God."

There can be no perfecting of saints without it, there can be no bride of Christ without it. It is easy to sprinkle with water, it is easy to eat the bread and drink the wine, it is easy to sing the psalm and chant the hymn, it is easy to wear the garb and say the phrase, it is easy to pray with the lips and to speak words; but the finished Christian is known by the love which suffereth long and is kind, which beareth all things, believeth all things, hopeth all things, endureth all things—and that is hard to attain. It comes not by an easy method. It comes not from the laying on of hands, it is not given as a prize for strict orthodoxy, nor for eagerness in pursuing what is new, it is no gift of priest or church.

It is the fruit of being born of God, it is the perfume which comes from a transformed life, it is the glorious sign that a human life has been changed until it has received the mark of the divine nature—love ; for God is Love. It is not puffed up, it is not provoked, it vaunteth not itself, it seeketh not its own ; it constructeth, it cements, it unifies, it vitalizes. Christians are told to love even as Christ loved ! If they once fulfilled this command they would become an irresistible spiritual power, and the realm of the King would widen beyond all conception. This is "the more excellent way," and yet we try every other way instead !

CHAPTER VIII

THE GIFT OF LISTENING TO GOD

DEAF children are always dumb. It is not possible for a child to speak human language until he has heard it spoken. We speak *because* we have heard. The same law is true in spiritual things. It is not possible to communicate until we have heard. The great voices that "cry" to our generation, or to any other generation, the men that are reaching the ears and the hearts of the people, the message-bearers of our time, or of any other time, must first have listened and heard. The word "prophet" means one who "speaks for" God. A prophet is dumb until he hears God; he opens his lips only when he hears.

These are very old truths, and probably everybody agrees that they are true *in the abstract*, but yet they are very much ignored and neglected *in fact*. It seems to us that one of the supreme gifts conferred upon man is the gift of listening to God, but it is a gift that is sadly neglected, and through this neglect the spiritual life of the individual and of the church suffers loss.

There has been among the Friends a strong reaction from "silent meetings" because they proved lifeless and profitless to most persons. They seemed dead and formal to all but an elect few, and meetings where there were no vital messages slowly diminished until they ceased to be. The result was that the pendulum swung to the opposite extreme, as so often happens, and silence became " a byword and a hissing," and a synonym for deadness and conservatism. Then, too, there was a practical difficulty. The times of silence gave occasion for all the unbalanced and undesirable speakers "to free their minds" at the expense of the patient congregation. The easy remedy seemed to be to have the time " filled " either with singing or with " profitable speaking." The result is that "the meeting for worship" which our fathers knew is going out of existence, and in its place we are getting "preaching meetings," "prayer meetings," "praise meetings" and "testimony meetings." The great fact remains that there is no greater gift than the gift of listening to God, and that there is no greater spiritual power than that which comes when a whole congregation is fused and melted in silent waiting and soul worship before the living God, when God's presence can be felt and His voice heard so distinctly that no audible words are needed.

There is nothing the Christian Church more needs than such living, convincing worship, and such times of holy hush before the Father of spirits, but it is apparently becoming a "lost gift," and there are many Friends who do not believe there is anything in silence. Of course there is not anything in empty silence, nor is there anything in empty speaking, but it is certain that we shall never get prophets until we learn to listen, and we shall never get mighty, convincing messages which make the congregation vibrate like "harps of God" until we learn to worship together in living silence. Nobody wants to see formal silent meetings. Every congregation needs ministry, teaching, exhortation, interpretation; but the speaker should speak because he has heard, and he should make his hearers realize that he has *listened* before his lips moved. We have an abundance of prayers in our meetings, and we have much that is properly called worship, but we believe that a new power would come in most of our congregations if we could increase in every member the gift of listening to God, and if every meeting could have seasons of hush and of united worship undisturbed by human voices. While we are eager to cultivate the gifts of utterance, as is fitting, let us by no means neglect the gift of listening to God.

CHAPTER IX.

THE MISSION OF THE CHURCH

IT is plainly evident that many Christians, perhaps most, do not yet begin to realize the full extent of the mission of the church to the world, and some do not seem to comprehend that it has any mission at all. The church? "Why it exists for its own members; it is the congregation of the faithful." The church? "It is an organization for guarding and preserving the heritage of spiritual truth committed to it." The church? "It is the ark of safety in the world for the salvation of the few who flee into it." "Its mission is to keep itself pure and true to its faith; to maintain a high standard; to add to its number such as are *suitable* to be members, and to preserve in the earth some representatives of its founder."

These are some of the inadequate conceptions which find expression among Christians. The church will never be greatly effective until its membership is possessed with Christ's idea of its mission. In His mind the body of believers are organic with Himself, branches of one vine, members of one body, with precisely the same mission He had. They are revealers of God to men. They are the light in the world as He is the Light of the world. No less a task than interpreting Christ to the whole human race devolves upon the church.

Something is wrong when a company of worshippers meet week after week to enjoy communion with the Lord, and sit unconcerned about the multitudes who in the same city live in misery, in hunger, in squalor, in vice and in sin. The contrasts of society are too great, and while they are so great there can be no honorable ease in the church, no excusable pride in its own purity and orthodoxy. "Ye say, 'Lord, Lord,' but ye do not my will," is the condemnation. There are people all about us who have no idea of what LOVE is. They have never had any love. It is only a word to them. They have never had human love enough to understand what Divine Love could be. If Christ is ever to become a reality to these people, and be a power in their lives, His spirit must first reach them through a human face and in the loving service of human hands.

The church has a twofold service towards such souls. It must take up the task of reforming the evils of a social system which makes such lives possible in the midst of our boasted civilization, and its members must take upon themselves the responsibility of interpreting Christ and the Christ-spirit to these sin-environed lives.

The tramp who crawls up to the back door for his unearned meal, and the drunkard who reels home to turn a family circle into an earthly hell, are both products of our social system, and there can be no pious ease for the church until such a system is destroyed. But this same tramp and this same drunkard might have made good, steady, valuable citizens if at the critical periods of their lives they had had some loving attention and uplifting influence, and had been made to feel that there was a better life within their reach. It is a fact that we always feel ourselves helpless to do anything to meet the hard situations that confront us in society as at present constituted, but it would be something gained if Christians could be made to realize that these are tasks which really belong to the church; that its mission is more than teaching orthodoxy and holding up a pure standard of membership. Christ had the reputation of associating with publicans and sinners, and with wine-bibbers. It was His mission to show the Divine life to these people, and to make their old life forever impossible afterwards. Our mission to-day should be as wide as His was, and all the sadness and hopelessness and sin about us should make it forever impossible for us to rest in the satisfaction and joy over our own salvation. The church must become Christ's BODY that His Spirit may finish the work of human redemption.

CHAPTER X

COMING TO GOD—THE ATONEMENT AS A PRACTICAL TRUTH

IT will be admitted by everybody, we believe, that God's revelation of Himself, His dealings with us, and the death on the Cross, all have one end in view—to bring men to God. God sent forth His son that we might become sons. No simpler or clearer statement of the Divine movement for man's redemption can be made than that. This is the problem—man has sinned, has followed his own will, has put himself away from God, and has made himself an alien. How shall he get back to God and realize that the enmity is past, and that he is *made* a son? We are speaking now wholly of the problem from our human point of view, which is, in the deepest and truest sense, a practical one. God's method was to show Himself and reveal His love, and thus to draw men to Him. He came to us as a Person, and spoke in human terms. He wrought with human hands. He lived a perfect life in the midst of sin and temptation. He illustrated the meaning of life on the highest spiritual level. He showed the significance and power of sacrifice and sympathy. He *fulfilled* all that was partial and incomplete in the past. He was Emanuel— God with us—in such a real and literal sense that those who saw Him saw God, and those who knew Him knew the Father's will.

But the most of those who saw and heard refused to believe; they did not go through him to God. They asked for impossible signs. They failed to see in him the fulfillment of Scripture and prophecy, and the holy ideals of the race. The mere showing of Himself as Life and Light did not draw them to God. There was one supreme step which remained. He could die for men and pour out his love with His life. If that failed to reach human hearts nothing could reach them. But he believed it would not fail. "I, if I be lifted up shall draw all men unto myself." He gave Himself. He gave Himself solely for others. His dying was in every sense vicarious. He took upon Himself the whole burden of sin, and He bore it for us. But He did it that we henceforth might see, in this crucified Christ, the length and breadth and depth and height of God's love, and that we might be drawn by it to forsake all sin, and come to Him for the new life of sonship. Speaking still on the human side, the atonement is made when Christ brings us to God by this gift of Himself. When a soul living in sin and an alien from God, and under comdemnation, realizes that Christ died for him, and that that loving heart is seeking for him, and drawing him from sin to sonship; and his own heart is touched, so that he sets his face, through love to this Christ, to begin a new life as a child of God, he gains an immediate sense of the practical meaning of the atonement which is worth more than a thousand volumes of theological discussion on the subject.

So far the subject is clear and plain. Christ came and died that he might draw us to God. When we yield to the drawing we become *as one* with God. "We know that we are of God," and "we know that the Son of God has come."

There is nothing metaphysical or mystical here, nothing which a child who has once felt the power of a mother's love cannot appreciate and respond to. It comes as a holy message to anyone who realizes the defects of sin and the power of evil habit. It is an announcement of a greater power—the power of God unto salvation to everyone that believes. It is as practical and as much related to the needs of our lives as the bread for our body, or the light for our eyes.

Far be it for us to imply that we can fathom or describe all the meaning of That Life and That Death. We would not take the rough tools of scientific investigation into Gethsemane or to Calvary to report that there is no mystery there which we have not explored. We do not understand entirely the meaning and significance of any life or any death. The moment we try we are beyond our depth. What this sacrifice, this crucifixion, meant on the Divine side, or what place it had in the eternal Nature, is not our question or our concern, and we do not wish to explore it or pronounce upon it. Our Gospels are silent on these metaphysical questions, and deal everywhere with Christ's practical purposes, viz., " to give men life, and to give it in abundant measure." It is life, not theory, which brought the Son of God to us. Life and not speculation is His gift to us now.

This practical, positive meaning is as clear as the sky above us; God's method of bringing men to himself culminated in a Personal coming, and that coming culminated in an agony and a death. This Divine movement to bring men to God is the supreme appeal to human hearts, and its significance as an atonement with God is realized positively by those who respond to it and find peace.

CHAPTER XI

HEART, SOUL, STRENGTH, MIND

IT is always well to consider carefully how Christ dealt with inquirers, for His method of solving religious difficulties must be our guide in similar situations. There are many instances recorded where He talked with seekers, and all these passages are full of illumination. He never speaks as a theologian, as though with a logical phrase he could help a hungry soul, but He always goes straight to the heart of the situation with a few vital words which are just as fresh and true and satisfying to-day as when they were first spoken.

Take the case of the young lawyer with the right Scripture passages always at his tongue's end. He wants to know how to "inherit eternal life." He soon learns that eternal life is not "inherited" as ancestral lands or government bonds are. It comes not by right of elder sonship or family connection. It is no heirloom for certain privileged families.

The Master makes His questioner give the right answer with his own lips. "What are the conditions to eternal life?" "Thou shalt love the Lord thy God with all thy HEART, and with all thy SOUL, and with all thy STRENGTH, and with all thy MIND, and thy neighbor as thy self." This is of course no complete theological definition of the plan of salvation, but it is a practical statement of the conditions of eternal life. What a comprehensive sweep it is! and what a message of breadth it has for some of us narrow, modern Christians!

We have just been listening to a sermon against "creaturely activity,"—a plea for passive waiting on the Lord. We hear again and again that the mind, *i. e.*, the intellect, the thought, must be repressed in order that the soul may commune with God, and we not seldom listen to solemn cautions against the emotions of the heart. In fact, too many persons think that to be religious one must kill out or suppress most of the faculties of the being. Not so the Master. He has a use for every part of the nature. He tells His questioner that if he wants to come into eternal life he must have heart, soul, strength, mind vibrating with love to God and to man. Afraid of "creaturely activity"! fearful lest the heart shall swell and grow warm! timorous above thought! Why, Christ says that the very condition of entering eternal life is to love with the heart, love with the soul, love with the strength, the physical activities, love with the powers of the mind. This means that these faculties of our being are to turn toward Him as the flower turns toward the sun, and let their activities move in joyous accord and harmony with His will.

It is impossible to keep a healthy child from activity; the life within it makes it active. Tie its hands and fetter its activities and you kill it by slow process. It is impossible for a genuinely religious being to keep from spiritual activity. Its mind is after truth, its heart is warm with love for Him who has loved even to death, its strength is consecrated to the service of lifting others, its soul is responsive to the Will of the Spirit. We do not forget that Christ has many things to say to one who is seeking eternal life, but this is His first word, His practical answer, "Love with the whole being. Let God have and tune every power and faculty until their activities move rythmically to His will."

CHAPTER XII

A POSTPONED HEAVEN

IT is not easy to talk or write on the "doctrine" or "experience" of holiness so that anybody else shall be satisfied with what we say. In fact it is very much like trying to give a good definition of "Love," or of "Life." When we approach these supreme subjects the best we can do is to stammer out our meaning, and we either say too little or too much.

There surely has been a good deal of unwise teaching on this subject, as there has on almost every phase of spiritual experience, but that ought not to blind our eyes to the real fact— the mighty truth—that Jesus Christ expects *us* to be complete in Him, and that the burden of His prayer,—which Christians of all ages have used,—is that God's will may be done in earth EVEN AS it is in heaven.

It is certainly true that the Christian standard has been kept too low rather than too high. Most Christians apparently never imagine that they are expected to be "perfect." They quote the old proverbs glibly: "To err is human," "man is as prone to err as the sparks to fly upward," and they conclude that the line of life is bound to be a wavy one, full of bends and curves—never straight onward. They believe that this world is a vale of sin; it is no place for white robes and palm branches, and triumphant songs. These will come only when we get to the heaven beyond the stars, and temptations no more assail us. Heaven is always postponed; it is a place always hoped for, never realized.

It is our personal opinion that this "easy creed," this low standard, this postponement of heavenly joys, is just the reason why the church has no more spiritual power in this present world. He who expects little, gets little; he who thinks that Christian life is bound to be streaked with black and white like a checker board, will of course never rise beyond that kind of life, and he who never realizes that Christ's purpose is to make a "new creature," can only testify that "the kingdom of heaven is at hand," he can never say, "the kingdom of heaven HAS COME!"

There are dangers of course when mortal, human beings go around declaring themselves to be "above sin," "free from law," and "perfect," but all this comes from misunderstanding what holiness is. Holiness is perfect love of God's will, and a perfect determination to live in His will. It does not take the Christian out of this world, it does not make him infallible, it does not relieve him of temptation, it does not make him a law unto himself, it does not allow him to boast of his sinlessness or his spiritual power.

It is simply a condition of heart into which Christ brings His disciples, where sin is hated and God's will is chosen, so far as it is known, above everything else. Love becomes the law of life, and the soul realizes that heaven is not a remote place, but a present fact. The kingdom of heaven has come wherever the King holds sway. This is no impossible doctrine, it is no experience reserved for a few rare saints. It is the privilege and should be the attainment of us all.

CHAPTER XIII

WROUGHT FOR THIS SELF-SAME THING

WHAT does God mean and what can His purpose be, or is it some enemy who has done this? Thus we stand and question in the presence of the inscrutable mystery which settles down over our lives and shuts out from our sight all that is dearest and best to us. It is the old, old question, rising occasionally into Abraham's complaint, "Dost thou well, Lord?" But no one who really believes in God can long blindly question or sit complaining in cold sackcloth and ashes. There must be an *answer*, if God is God, and He cannot mock us or leave us with no voice of Hope.

The real answer is one which goes down into the very heart of the mystery of *life*, and grasps its purpose, for we cannot fathom death until we fathom life. Paul puts his finger on the nerve of it when he says that mortality shall be swallowed up of life and God hath wrought us for this self-same thing. With God, mortality is only an incident in the life-process. It is a brief stopping-place, a hostelry, on the way to a less unencumbered life. It is just our chance at the prize of learning love; it is our opportunity for becoming distinct, individual selves and of being shaped into the image of God. Mortality is not an end in itself, it is not an absolute good. It is only a tent to be used while the house is being made; it is only a means to an end which is beyond; it is not the height, but the ladder by which the height is reached. At length life swallows up mortality, as the growing, winged creature within bursts the chrysalis and mounts up to its new sphere. It is only as we bend over the empty chrysalis that we cry out, "An enemy hath done this," or "hast thou done well, Lord?" When we lift our eyes and vision returns, we see that there is no break in the infinite, loving purpose, and we hear Him say again, "It was wrought for this self-same thing; to be clothed upon that mortality might be swallowed up of life." Life is not dependent upon any one particular expression of itself; it is rich in means and in forms. What seem to us breaks and chasms are only invisible links in an unbroken chain, hidden arcs in an ever-renewed and vital process and movement which is fed continually by the one source and fountain of all life. When we look down and think of our side, it is all loss and mystery; when we look up and think of the Divine purpose, it is all light and victory. If God *is* Love, then so surely He hath wrought us to be clothed upon, and mortality is swallowed up of life.

CHAPTER XIV

NO SIGN SHALL BE GIVEN

THERE is but one occasion on record which drew a deep sigh of discouragement from the heart of Jesus. Twice He wept; once in sympathy with mourners, though not in hopeless grief, because He was conscious at the same time that He was the resurrection and the life, and again over Jerusalem, because He saw that only on the ruins of the Jerusalem He loved could the more perfect Jerusalem arise. But this "deep sigh" was different. It was called out by a hopeless situation which came before Him in His ministry. The people who failed to feel the power of the truth He taught, and were incapable of appreciating His spiritual revelation, came demanding that He should authenticate or prove His revelation by a physical "sign." "He sighed deeply and said, 'No sign shall be given.'" In fact, from the nature of the case no sign could be given. Spiritual truth must be taken at first-hand or not at all. No physical sign could be given to prove, or authenticate Christ's message of

Divine love, of forgiveness of sin, of sonship with God, or the possibility of a life hid with Christ in God.

One of Christ's severest temptations was the suggestion that He should miraculously make bread for Himself out of stone. It was a temptation to use His marvelous powers, but it threatened His very Messiahship, for if He had yielded He could have brought no redemption to man. If bread is made out of stones by a miracle for Him who comes as a Saviour of men, it at once puts Him out of relations with those whom He came to save. We must toil and struggle, and eat our bread in the sweat of our brows, and if He refuses to taste man's hardship and want, and eats the bread of miracle, He ceases to be in all points like us, and, not sharing our life, He cannot be our complete Redeemer. He could not yield and still be the Saviour.

The impossibility of yielding to the cry for a physical miraculous "sign" is made still clearer during the crucifixion. The mocking priests and scribes ask for a last sign: "If He be the Christ, let Him come down from the cross that we may believe." It was the very thing which would have proved Him no Christ at all. The gift of Himself, the manifestation of Divine love, His faithfulness unto death did prove His Sonship and attest His message, but the sign they demanded was forever impossible for Him, who even on the cross proves His spiritual power, not by coming down Himself, but by lifting a dying thief out of his old, ruined life, up, up, until he sees the meaning of love and sonship, and can BE WITH CHRIST in paradise.

This power to transform a life, and bring it into Divine relation, is the supreme sign; it is the only sign by which Christ could attest His spiritual message. Magdalen is a "sign;" Simon, the wavering, fickle, impetuous fisherman, changed to Peter, the apostle of Jesus Christ is a sign; John, the son of thunder, wishing to call down fire on the Samaritans, transformed into the apostle of love, is a sign; Saul, breathing out threatenings and slaughter, hauling men and women to prison, changed to Paul with his life hid with Christ in God, who, also "crucified with Christ," can say in truth, "I live by the faith of the Son of God, who loved me and gave himself for me," he is a sign. Every soul since, which through Christ has turned from its prodigal life, and cried, "Abba, Father," has found Christ's truth true, and has become a living sign to others. No other sign shall be given to this or any other generation.

Each generation in its own way asks for a sign. Crowds gather around the spiritualistic "medium" to get a material "sign" that the soul lives after death, but not thus shall the great truth of immortality be proved. One generation expects the astronomer with his telescope to find an indisputable sign in the starry heavens; another asks the geologist to dig up one from the strata of the earth's crust, or the biologist to find a sign in the cells of living forms. It is because of the failure to find God in material things that a modern poet has cried out in hopelessness:

> "The God I never once behold,
> Above the cloud, beneath the clod;
> The unknown God, the unknown God."
>
> —WILLIAM WATSON.

The trouble is, he is looking in the wrong direction for Him, and he is asking for a sign which cannot be given. "God is love," let us remember, and He can be *found* only where love can be, and the sign must be sought in a human heart that can feel and test a spiritual truth.

That is the meaning of Tennyson's great lines in "In Memoriam," written when his own heart was yearning for a sign that God is love and that life goes on. He says:

"I found him not in world or sun,
    In eagle's wing or insect's eye;
    Nor thro' the questions men may try,
The petty cobwebs we have spun.

"If e'er when faith hath fallen asleep
    I heard a voice, 'Believe no more'
    And heard an ever-breaking shore
That tumbled in the Godless deep;

"A warmth within the breast would melt
    The freezing reason's colder part,
    And like a man in wrath, the heart
Stood up and answered, 'I HAVE FELT.'"

This first-hand knowledge, by experience-is the only all-sufficient attestation of a spiritual truth, and however much we may long for tests through our senses, and for signs that are tangible, we must at last get where we can receive His beatitude, "blessed are they that have not yet seen, yet have believed," and cry out, because our hearts know Him, "my Lord and my God."

CHAPTER XV

PISGAH VIEWS OF LIFE

"Now I see all of it,
Only I'm dying!"

WHAT lives we might live if we could only begin life with the wisdom which we shall possess when we stand at its close, and look back on it and realize that our earthly opportunities are at an end! How trivial much of one's life must seem viewed from its farther end, and how strenuous and earnest it would be if it could be lived over in the light of the experience which these closing moments bring! It is not well to be haunted by the shadow of death, and it is an indication of an unhealthy and morbid condition; but it might be well occasionally, if we could take Pisgah views of life, and see it—see our own lives—in what the philosophers call an "eternal aspect."

Most of us live for the hour; we do what pleases us at the time. We see a pleasure or a task close at hand, and we enjoy the one and brace ourselves to perform the other, and we live largely as the creatures of circumstance, having our lives shaped by the things and the persons about us. Some of us toil and struggle with work and poverty and daily cares until life seems one long grind and death a happy release; others of us dabble and play with questions and problems, and lose sight of the great clear truths which we ought to see; still others of us refuse the drudgery of life, with its strenuous burdens, and devote ourselves to catching phantoms and ghosts while the real, serious things of life are neglected. How all this would be changed if we could really see the meaning of life as it will break upon us at the extreme verge! We all know how some great hope or purpose suddenly changes— transforms our life, and makes the work or the pleasures become totally different things. Work is no longer hard because its brings us nearer our fixed hope and purpose; frivolous pleasures become hateful to us, for they hinder us in the pursuit of our goal; the petty things that used to vex are brushed away with unconcern, because the vision of our realized hope is full upon us, and obliterates the little shadows which we used to know. Much more would life readjust itself, and the pettiness of it vanish if we could enter it with our eyes full of the "eternal aspect;" if we could keep with us some foregleams of the Pisgah view. A modern poet has given a remarkable picture of Lazarus after his return from the grave with the new meaning of life revealed to him, a few lines of which we give:

> " He holds on firmly to some thread of life
> Which runs across some vast distracting orb
> Of glory on either side that meagre thread,
> Which, conscious of, he must not enter yet—
> THE SPIRITUAL LIFE AROUND THE EARTHLY LIFE:
> The law of that is known to him as this,
> His heart and brain move there, his feet stay here."

Now there is such a thing as getting the gaze so fixed on the celestial city that the things of earth are neglected, and of getting so full of visions and dreams that plain, everyday duties and joys are ignored. We write no word to encourage anybody in that mistaken course, but we would emphasize the truth that daily life and daily tasks and duties should be transfigured with foregleams of a light upon them from the eternal day which will break in fullness on the Pisgah heights of life.

CHAPTER XVI

THE VINE-STOCK

CHRISTIANITY is a religion of thought; it is a religion of faith; it is a religion of belief; it is a religion of love, but above everything else it is a religion of life. It is not enough to think correctly; it is not enough to believe rightly; it is not even enough to love deeply. The first question is one of life. "If any man BE IN CHRIST, he is a new creature." It all turns on that one question, and this distinguishes Christianity from every other religion on the globe. The New Testament has a hundred ways of saying this supreme fact of Christianity, and yet we often fail to realize how it underlies the whole method of salvation. *Union with Christ, and not an opinion about Christ*, is what we mean.

It is all told in one beautifully clear figure of our Master: "I am the vine-stock, ye are the branches." Spiritual life, and all that flows from it, begins when a soul comes into vital and organic relations with the living Christ, and there is no possible substitute for such a vital union, Paul at once fixed upon this as the central truth of Christianity, and he put it in one form or another before all the churches he established. Ask Paul what makes a man a Christian, and you will hear him say, "To be in Christ." He never thinks of salvation as something which goes on in a man's head, as the acceptance of certain formulas or "views." He is not interested in dried and pressed specimens of truth. For him truth is always a living thing with its currents flowing and its fruit ripening.

We now know that it is impossible to think a single thought without a flow of blood to the brain, and we also know that it is impossible to get the blood without putting food into the system. The grain of wheat, the piece of beef, must be organic in the brain before we can think our thought, and it must be organic in the muscle before we can put forth our strength of arm. Until Christ is in a man's life and organic with his deepest self —not remote in time or space—the man is not in the truest sense a Christian.

The dynamo does not *make* electricity; it only furnishes a medium for electrical force to work through. The electricity is in the dynamo, though it did not originate there. A Christian is merely a medium for Christ, and the work begins and the power appears when Christ is in the man. The end and purpose of life is to " grow up into Him in all things."

CHAPTER XVII

THE PLACE OF THE HOME IN CIVILIZATION

THE Christian home is the highest product of civilization; in fact, there is nothing that can be called civilization where the home is absent. The savage is on his way out of savagery and barbarity as soon as he can create a home and make family life at all sacred. The real horror of the "slums" in our great cities is that there are no homes there, but human beings crowded indiscriminately into one room. It is the real trouble with the "poor whites" of the South that they have failed to preserve the home as a sacred centre of life. One of the first services of the foreign missionary is to help establish homes among the people whom he hopes to Christianize. In short, the home is the true unit of society. It determines what the individual shall be, it shapes the social life, it makes the church possible, it is the basis of the state and nation. A society of mere individual units is inconceivable. Men and women, each for self, and with no holy centre for family life, could never compose either a church or a state.

Christianity has created the home as we know it, and this is its highest service to the world, for the kingdom of heaven would be realized if the Christian home were universal. The mother's knee is still the holiest place in the world, and the home life determines more than any other one influence, and perhaps more than all influences combined, what the destiny of the boy or girl shall be.

We may well rejoice in the power of the Sabbath School, the Christian ministry, the secular school, the college, the university, but altogether they do not measure up to the power of the homes, which are silently, gradually determining the future lives of those who will compose the Sabbath School, the church, the school and the college.

The woman who is successful in making a true home, where peace and love dwell, and in which the children whom God gives her feel the sacredness and holy meaning of life, where her husband renews his strength for the struggles and activities of his life, and in which all unite to promote the happiness and highest welfare of each other—that woman has won the best crown there is in this life, and she has served the world in very high degree. The union of man and woman for the creation of a home breathing an atmosphere of love is Christ's best parable of the highest possible spiritual union where the soul is the bride and He is the Eternal Bridegroom and they are one.

CHAPTER XVIII

THE ETERNAL NATURE OF THINGS

THERE is a strong tendency in our day toward what is sometimes called a "soft" or "easy" theology. The harsh and fear-inspiring features are eliminated, and we hear little of the old-time theology which made the world to come such a stern reality. We are told of the love which woos and forgives, until we almost, or quite, forget that there is anything to fear. If God is love, indeed, we are told, why should there be anything to fear? and we hear the question asked, Were not the threats and the terrors for an age which could not comprehend a God of love, and which needed to be frightened into goodness? and has not the time come for an easier religion, stripped of all aspects of terror and harshness? We do not profess to be able to say what the Allwise One will do with this particular soul or that, when it comes into that world which lies so entirely beyond our experience, nor are we authorized to "speak for our Creator;" but we believe that our so-called "soft theology" of modern times is not true to the nature of things, nor does it square with the revelations which have been given of God's nature and His purposes.

An ancient Hebrew poet says that "the stars in their courses fought against Sisera,"—the very nature of things were against him. In fact, every page of history gives us a stern lesson of the futility and impossibility of ignoring the distinction of right or wrong— righteousness and unrighteousness. It is one long story of men and women who "dashed up against the thick bossed shield of God's judgment," and who were broken against this impenetrable shield.

Nature has the same story to tell. You must learn her laws and obey them, or suffer for it. She is never "easy" with those who will not learn her ways. The unplumb building topples over, the rotten foundation brings the structure down, the badly built scaffolding crashes down, regardless of who gets hurt. The ship which is not steered by compass and chart grinds to pieces on the reefs, unmindful of the precious lives aboard; and the train, as we learn this morning, which comes behind time and finds the track blocked, crashes into the obstruction, careless of how many are killed. There is nothing "soft" in the eternal nature of things, if so be we blindly dash against things as they are. The only safe and wise way is to adjust one's course to fit the nature of things, otherwise the punishment comes irresitibly.

Why, in the light of this, or in the light of anything else, should we suppose that all will come out right, no matter how we shape our lives? It will not come out right. Evil is *not* good, however we juggle with names, and God cannot be God and treat unrighteousness, or even carelessness, as though it made no difference.

Does anybody suppose that love is "soft" and devoid of sternness. The father who loves his child the most is the one who is most afraid to be "easy" with him when he is on the wrong course. It is just because God is love that He is also "a consuming fire." It is not possible that the stubborn, the willful, the erring, the vicious, or even the thoughtless, should go on "in their ways" forever. It would destroy all the purpose and meaning of the universe. The universe makes for righteousness, and those who will not learn this fact by easy methods must have harsh methods,—"the thick bossed shield of God's judgment."

> "The tissues of the life to be
>   We weave with colors all our own,
> And in the field of destiny
>   We reap as we have sown."

CHAPTER XIX

DIVERSIONS AND RECREATIONS

WAS there ever a Christian outside the monastery, who did not have to ask at some time in his life, "What kind of diversion is consistent with my Christian profession?" Was there ever a Christian parent who did not find it hard to know just where to draw the line of permissions and prohibitions for the unformed boy or girl?

Every growing person, perhaps every person, needs some recreation, some relaxation from the strain of work, some diversion from strenuous life. It is a necessity to good, healthy, genuine living, and without it the sap of life dries up and the man becomes like a machine. Alternation is woven everywhere in the Divine plan for the universe. Ebb and flow, day and night, summer and winter, joy and sorrow, toil and refreshment are involved in the structure of things.

Take away the recreation and the periods of unbending and you cut the nerve of genuine effort and shrivel the muscles of toil. But on the other hand almost every form of recreation and diversion is open to abuse, and some forms lead to positive immorality. We must have the world to live in, and we have to use it for our needs; but we find at once that it often soils where we touch it, and that too often, when we go to it for recreation, it takes advantage of us and unmakes rather than recreates us. So that it becomes a difficult problem to find proper diversion without at the same time carrying away upon us the dark touch-spots of the world. Every game can be gambled with, every harmless pastime may be pushed to a dangerous extreme, and joyous play may lead to an unsuspected sin. There is nothing on earth that is not open to excess, and the pleasure-seeker is always walking a path beset with pitfalls and intersected at every point with bye-paths, which lead gradually into real sins.

It may do some good to mark out a few forms of recreation as peculiarly bad and dangerous, and to warn all Christians away from them, and there are certain diversions and amusements which must be prohibited to the young while they are undeveloped and immature. But the only real remedy for this difficulty which we are discussing is the development of a strong spiritual life and a genuine moral character. A person will eventually sag down and drift into a low and harmful form of diversion if he has not cultivated a taste for something higher and purer. You cannot keep people out of sin in this world by preaching sensational sermons against certain forms of evil, while sometimes the very description of the evil kindles a desire to try it. The only way to keep a boy out of the lurking traps of sin is to get him in love with something holy, and get his soul set upon a high aim and a true life. He must be made to feel that there is no pleasure or recreation in anything that makes him less manly, and pure, or that interferes at all in his purpose for life. The best way to steer a young person through the dangers attending recreation is to help him see the positive side of life, and go to work to help him put on the whole armor of God, that he may withstand in the evil day. The formation of spiritual character—putting on Christ literally—is the only sure way to be ready to meet the open doors to forbidden pleasures, and this is the first business of every Christian parent and of every Christian church.

CHAPTER XX

A RELIGION OF POWER

THERE have been many ways of regarding religion, and different persons to-day think of it differently. It is very common to speak of it as some thing which one "gets" or "accepts." "He got religion," the neighbors say, or "he has always kept his religion through every trial." It is not uncommon to think of it as a statement of belief or faith which a person holds. "I accept the doctrine of the Trinity, of the atonement, and of eternal life, and eternal punishment, therefore I have religion;" thus many a person explains his religion. To such a one it consists largely of correct definitions. Another class of persons care nothing for definition; they consider religion to be a good life; they say: "I do about right, I live up to my light and I do not believe God will be hard on me."

There is still another way of viewing religion. It is the power of God manifested in life. It does not begin with definitions, it does not consist of living about right, it is not something one "gets." It comes and gets the person. He does not keep his religion, but his religion keeps him. It is a power, a force, just as real and just as persistent as that which we call gravitation, and its effects are just as sure. No definitions of electricity would ever light a man's house, or move a trolley car. The first step is to let the current in and the house becomes light, or the car moves. Everything bases itself on the ultimate, invisible power, which is simply RECEIVED. This is true of religion as it is of mechanics. There is no religion apart from God, and until a man comes to God and God gets him, the man is not truly religious. It consists first and last of possession—God's possession of us and our joy in the sense of His ownership. A religion without power would be like a gravitation which did not draw anything, or like electricity that had no force. Religion is spiritual gravitation. It draws the soul away from everything else to its true Central Sun. The first effect of it on a person is to beget love. Love is the unfailing sign of religion. A loveless religion is as impossible as a waterless ocean, or a treeless forest. If a man's religion does not flood him with love, it is the wrong kind of religion.

We have been speaking of what religion seems to us to be, now a word about how it comes. There has been in our world but one Person who was perfectly divine and perfectly human. He revealed God and He showed what it means to be a son. He also showed how to be a son, and he plainly said to the whole race, "I am the Way." Religion means getting to God, Christ is the way and love is the sign.

CHAPTER XXI

PENTECOST IN OUR CHRISTIANITY

PENTECOST was a definite date and a definite experience in the early church. It came fifty days after the crucifixion, and the second chapter of Acts gives us all the information we have of the event, as there is no other reference to it in the New Testament.

So far as we know, much that occurred on that particular day has never been repeated. There were visible and audible phenomena which nobody can now clearly explain and which are generally considered to have been a special dispensation for the benefit of the little group of believers who had it laid upon them to carry the Gospel to an unbelieving world.

The one feature of Pentecost which is as possible for us to-day as for apostles and friends of Jesus ten days after their Master had left their sight, is the reception of the Holy Ghost. We apparently do not need the gift of tongues, and the visible fire no longer sits on the head of a modern Christian. Every Christian does, however, need to have a consciousness of the presence of the Spirit of God, and not one of us can afford to miss the power which comes when the Divine Spirit breaks through a human life. All that was really vital in the Jerusalem Pentecost may be repeated in the experience of every Christian, and our belief is that no one can be at his best until the Spirit of God floods his life and makes him see that salvation is infinitely more than the mere escape from the just penalty of sin.

"He that is joined to the Lord is one Spirit," i.e., he who apprehends Christ and puts Him on, he whose life is hid with Christ, finds that his human spirit is taken up into the Divine Spirit and the Spirit-life becomes natural and habitual, but the Pentecost experience does not mean that Christ has gone and that we have gained something better. Christ is never gone out of the Christian's life. The very way to gain the full life of the Spirit is to be joined to the Lord; there is no other way to it. Those who profess to get beyond the morality and the teaching and the drawing of Christ into a state above law and order are sailing without chart or compass and are steering straight for the rocks.

We do not say that the minister needs a different kind of experience than the humblest member of the body. No attainable degree of life or of baptism is too good for the Christian with the one talent or the half of a talent, if they are ever divided. The ministers, the teachers, the evangelists, need a "gift" which perhaps the ordinary member does not have. We call a man a minister because we recognize his gift, but the man who picks stones in the field, who builds the house, who sits at the receipt of custom in the bank, needs to be filled with the fullness of God, as well as the minister does, to enable him to lead the overcoming life, which is after all the only true life. There is a striking difference between the diamond, the sapphire and the opal, but it is the same light which makes all three beautiful. We are all different in our make-up and character, but the thing which makes any Christian, in any walk of life, a man of power is his union with Christ, and his life in the Spirit. Whether we can tell of the rushing, mighty wind or not, we all ought to be able to show that the Spirit has come and has made Pentecost a present reality for us.

CHAPTER XXII

WORSHIPING GOD

THE Christian Church has made great progress in this century. The preaching of the Gospel is much more vital and convincing than at the beginning of the century, and there is a genuine effort apparent to apply Christianity to all the problems of real life rather than to discuss metaphysical and unknowable questions which only perplex the listeners and leave them farther from the heart of God. The Church has been gradually awakening to the needs of the unsaved part of society whether at home or in foreign fields, and a more effective missionary work has been done in this century than in any since the days of the primitive Church. In no other age of the world, either ancient or modern, has the Bible received such thorough and intelligent study. Not only are the millions of children studying it, but every thoughtful Christian, whether a profound scholar or not, studies this Book, and it has become to us a more living message than in any other period of history, while every new discovery helps us understand it better. But while all this is true, it is perhaps doubtful if we are learning how to worship God more truly. In a certain sense all sincere service is worship, and all appreciation of God's goodness must be pleasing to Him whether expressed in words or in deeds, but there is a deeper worship which belongs to the life of every growing Christian. Neither singing, nor speaking, nor listening, nor doing, can take its place. It is a conscious sense of the Divine Presence enveloping us, and a response of the heart to His holy communing. No Christian life can be complete without these times of genuine intercourse with God.

When we pray we have our requests to make; we come seeking and asking; when we praise we give voice to our feelings of joy in his goodness, and when we witness we tell what He has done for us, but there are times when the soul needs to get deeper than any of these states.

The little child runs to the father expecting some present, and then he pours out his thanks for the pretty thing which he has brought, but there comes a time when the little heart learns that the father himself is better than any present, and that his love is more than a gift. So we come to learn that above everything else, we need just God. The soul that never comes directly to Him to enjoy His love will miss the deepest gift, and our manner of worship ought to provide for these occasions of true communion. The Friends have erred in the past in thinking that Christian life could progress best in prolonged silence, when really all Christians need teaching and expression for healthy progress, but it is a no less fatal mistake to suppose that worship must consist of vocal expression, and that Christian life can progress healthily without times of hush when God speaks to the congregation. The minister who rises to speak will have a new power if he and his hearers have just been hearing God speak before he rises, and it steadies and illumines every man to go down, or up, into God Himself, where requests cease and where the heart feels the pulsing of the Great Heart. This should not take the place of prayer or praise, or teaching, or service, or deeds, but this soul communion with God should be a part, and it is a necessary part, of true worship, for after all, the main purpose of a meeting is to make the members acquainted with God.

CHAPTER XXIII

CHRISTIANS IN THE WORLD

ONE of the earliest Christian writers after the apostolic days used to teach that Christians should be in the world what the soul is in the body. They are, according to this teaching, in the world not simply to perfect their own salvation, or to have rapturous experiences; they are here to fulfil a peculiar mission to the world. They are to give light to others who are still living in darkness, and they are to be as the salt of society, sweetening and "curing" the world.

That is a beautiful idea that Christians are to be in the world what the soul is to the body. We know only too well what happens to a body when the soul leaves it. Corruption and decay work away unhindered now the soul is gone. There is nothing left to repair the waste and to build up what the corrupting forces tear down.

When the soul goes out, we see at once that it never was the body we cared for; it was the invisible "self" which animated the body, and gave it expression and made it lovable. In fact, the real thing which makes a human being a being at all is the soul within it, and when this goes the body is nothing but a shell —a ruined chrysalis.

Now, what would the world be without Christians in it? We know what it used to be before ever there were Christians in it, and none of us would want to have a real experience of that kind of life. The French revolution is the most stupendous illustration of modern time of what the world easily becomes when Christianity is gone out of it. It corrupts, it decays, it teems with wickedness, and those who preach against Christianity and proclaim a Christless gospel would be horrified could they but see what the world would become when Christ was really gone, and Christians no longer remained to warm and sweeten life.

We know that Christians are imperfect enough; they come far short of their calling, but they, nevertheless, form the mightiest factor in modern civilization. Their influence reaches almost every corner of the world and every walk of life. When miners rush to the Arctic circle to wash gold from the frozen soil, Christian influences travel over the same mountain trail, and beautiful flowers of holiness and love bloom in sight of the tents of wickedness. Where the carcass is there are the eagles. Where corruption seems to poison the air, God's birds come to cleanse it. Oh, this is a great world, and God has not left it to putrify and "spoil." Sometimes it seems very bad and the smell of its sin shuts out all "odors of sanctity," but soon again the odors of a broken alabaster box reach us, and love proves mightier than sin. When shall we Christians learn that all true life is vicarious, that we are not here to storm at sin and to say, "Oh, Oh," at it, but to help put it down by doing in our sphere what our Master did in His sphere. We shall not die on crosses, and it would not help the world if we did, but beholding the spirit which was in Him who gave Himself in one great sacrifice for sin, let us realize that if we would complete the work which is left for us to do, we, too, must in a real sense, be crucified with Christ. The world does not care for our discussions of theology, and it laughs at our bickerings and hagglings and hair-splittings, but it acknowledges at once the conquering force of the true Christian life and unselfish love. Still, as in the second century, Christians are in the world what the soul is in the body.

CHAPTER XXIV

IF CHRIST CAME TO THE HOME

"SAY the word, for I am not worthy that Thou shouldst come under my roof." We can easily appreciate the centurion's modesty and his feeling that he was not worthy to have the Master come into his house; but is there not something besides humility in the request? Suppose that Christ should come unexpectedly into any of our homes and sit among us as our guest, would He find our homes all ready for His presence, or should we need to spend some months beforehand preparing for His coming? There were a few homes in Judea to which He went, though it is plainly evident that He did not feel at home in them all, as He did in the one at Bethany. He found much that had to be changed in Simon's house and in Zaccheus's house before He could abide there and be at home. Even in Bethany the odors from the broken alabaster box do not cover up the notes of strife between the sisters over the questions of service and housework.

The foxes had holes and the birds of the air had nests, but there was no home in Palestine for the Son of Man. We find Him praying on hill tops, in the wilderness, in the garden; never once in some harmonious, congenial family circle. We read again and again of His spending the night under the sky, generally alone; but never once of His being comfortably housed under a roof where loving hearts made the Great Burden Bearer feel that He was at home with them, and His cares and burdens lightened by sympathy. Perhaps He did find shelter and rest and loving sympathy and true communion in some unnamed homes in the so-called "Holy Land," but we can only imagine the scenes; they are not in the picture preserved for us. There is something peculiarly touching in the request of this old Roman soldier who wants his boy healed, but who is conscious that his home is not just the place for the Saviour to go to. The desired work is to be done, if possible, at long range. It is an old story. We go to the church or the meeting-house to meet the Lord, but too often we do not expect Him to come to our homes. Things are not in shape there for Him. We have our thousand perplexing home cares and fretting problems. We mean to be sweet and loving to each other; we know we ought to make our homes altars on which the vestal fires of love are never extinguished—but, but, but! Well, we fail to do it.

If Christ should come to-day we should probably want Him to help us at long range, at least until we could get the home fixed over so that He would not find it jarring upon His calm and peaceful spirit. Think what it means to have a home where Christ could rest and refresh Himself and of which He could say, as He began His journey again, "These same are My mother and My brothers and My sisters!"

CHAPTER XXV

CHRISTIANITY AND REFORM WORK

AS there is no conflict between religion and morals, so there is no conflict between philanthropic, or reform work, and Christianity. Some people are afraid of speaking much of *mere* morality for fear they are dishonoring religion by doing so, and in like manner it is felt by some that there is no place for mere reform work or philanthrophy, because it is on too low a plane, our business in this world being to preach Christ and His power to save, and that only.

There can be no doubt in the mind of any Christian that the all-important thing is to present to humanity the Saviour from sin, to induce as many as possible to yield to Him completely, and if they fully experience the cleansing, sanctifying power with which He fills a surrendered life, the questions of morality and of reform are settled so far as those lives are concerned, for in the acceptance of Christ, His standard of life must be adopted, or it is only a half-way step. While it must ever be the supreme thought with the ripe Christian to make it possible for men and women to become " new creatures," there can be no controversy with those who find it their mission to educate, to improve the condition of things by reform movements or by legislation, and who make life purer and easier by removing temptations and the causes of evil.

The half-taught disciples restrained those *casting out devils* because they did not follow the Master, but he rebuked them and gave them to understand that it was a victory for Him every time a devil was dethroned, in whatever way it was accomplished. " He that is not against us is for us." We often forget that broad teaching, and feel sometimes that the work must be done in our way or at least by those who have a like faith with us, or it cannot be a service for Christ; but His words are unmistakable, that no work which makes this a better world, which makes it easier for men to live a true life, is to be condemned. A defeat of Satan is a victory for Christ, a removal of the darkness means the incoming of the light; therefore, let us not relax any effort to work directly in His name for the salvation of the world through the Saviour, but let us have no word to say against any effort of individual or society for the overthrow of evil, or for the amelioration of suffering and the effects of sin. We can see how inconsistent it is to allow a cause to exist which makes the land abound with drunkards, paupers, criminals, and mentally incapacitated, but while it does exist we must find out how to deal wisely with those whom our imperfect civilization has wrecked. Meanwhile, we ought to devote all our powers, mental and moral, to the conception of some method that will forever remove the cause of the evil. The man or the woman, or the multitude, as the case may be,—who strikes successfully at this root of woe and ruin and crime, will have served God in *casting out devils*, whether it be done by a political method or a legal act, or by a campaign of education or on a definite religious basis. During the great crusade against slavery the work was interrupted by dissensions between the mere reformers and the churches. The churches would not work with the reformers because they did not put their opposition on a Christian basis, the reformers condemned the churches for not endorsing their methods. When Christ forgives us and makes us His He does not make us less truly, but more truly *men* than we were before. He does not call us apart from the problems of human improvement and progress. He puts us rather in the forefront of the great battle of Armageddon, and we are under orders "to ride abroad redressing human wrongs," to smite evil and sin and crime, and to aid the right and the truth. We have still living among us two valiant souls whom God has greatly blessed, a Moody and a Parkhurst. One has worked ceaselessly to bring men to Christ for salvation, the other has, with lance in hand, attacked the corruption and crime of his city. Both are knights of God, and they have no conflict with each other. The arrows of both are sharp in the heart of the King's enemies.

CHAPTER XXVI

OUR THOUGHT OF GOD

IT is an old and much-discussed question, whether it is our thought, or our will, or our emotions that determines our life, and makes us what we are. One man maintains that the "thought" is the root and spring of the whole being. "Only think right and the life will be all right." Another man finds this teacher entirely wrong, and concludes that the "feelings" are the main thing. "The life is shaped by the emotions, by what we care for, by what we love." "Oh! no," says the third man, "not at all. The life is determined by the choices you make, by your resolves, by your decisions, by what you WILL."

Now the mistake in all this comes from breaking the man up into three distinct parts and treating one of them as though it were the whole man. Thought and Will and Feeling never work singly or independently. They are all three together in all our acts and in all our life. They can no more be separated than the sky and air, or light and color can be separated.

The question has never been settled which one of these functions lies at the root of character, or of religious life, for it would be impossible to get a complete character or a genuine religious life with any one of the three functions gone. Anyone who has difficulty in comprehending the doctrine of the Trinity will find, if he looks at it, the same difficulty in comprehending how ONE SELF in his own nature can have three indissoluble, interwoven strands—in fact, three entirely different manifestations, which together make one consciousness.

But notwithstanding all this, we want still to emphasize the fact that it is tremendously important how a man THINKS. Wrong thought and wrong belief make imperfect lives every time. "My people will not think!" is Isaiah's constant burden.

Analyze an imperfect, weak, unproductive Christian life, and you will always find his thought of God is wrong, or at least very crude and imperfect. Let a man, on the other hand, once get his mind filled with Christ's conception of God, and his life begins to unfold and expand. It is like bringing a plant out of the cellar into the sunlight. Go back without any prejudices and preconceived ideas and see how simple Christ's idea of God is. He is a heavenly Father and His will is to have all His children like Himself. His kingdom comes wherever His will is done. True life consists in being about the Father's business. He is like the light which floods the earth, and He seeks to penetrate every dark spot. His heart is touched with all our burdens and sorrows, grieved over our errors and our waywardness, and He gives His own Son, His very self, to win us and draw us to Him. The essence of His nature is Love, and He reveals Himself and His Love that we may learn Love and so become like Him.

CHAPTER XXVII

THE FATHER AND THE SON

SOME of our friends have been much perplexed about the ever new question of the unity of Father and Son. If there is only one God, they ask, how can there be three persons? If there is only one God and Jesus Christ was God, then, when we say He died on the cross, does not that seem like saying that God died? which is an impossibility. Again, why should Christ need the Holy Ghost who descended upon Him, and what was the effect of this upon Him? Those who have studied the never-ending discussions on these speculations know how impossible it is to fathom the mystery of the Divine Nature, and they will feel as we do that in speaking at all on the subject one must do so with uncovered head and with no dogmatic confidence. We speak only that we may possibly help some, who are perplexed, to get a clearer idea of what revelation teaches us to think, and our words must be taken only in that sense, for a complete exposition would require a volume or a set of volumes.

There is but one God; we must hold fast to that truth. This God is Love. In our human thought, love implies a beloved object; therefore from eternity God generated the Son, who is the express image of His person. In the beginning, this expression of Himself existed —this Logos, which we translate Word. It is the self-revealing aspect of the Divine self. It is that in Him which can be manifested. We know that the undivided ray of light can without ceasing to be light or effulgence manifest itself as color; yet light and color are not two things but one. So Father and Son are not two essences, but ONE. This eternally generated manifestation of Himself,—this object of His love—in the fulness of time became incarnate, became flesh and dwelt among us, and we beheld in Him the glory of the only begotten Son. If God were to express Himself truly to human beings, He could do it only in a perfect human life, which should perfectly unite Divinity and humanity. Some persons refuse to think of Jesus Christ as really human at all; they think it destroys His divinity to think of Him so, and therefore they conceive of Him as only going through the motions of human life while He knew all the time that He was not human at all. This idea is entirely foreign to the Gospels and to the facts, and would make the incarnation unreal. He, the very God, became man. He lived a perfect human life. He learned by experience as we all have to do. He suffered privations. He felt and deeply tasted the hard realities of slighted love, of disappointed hopes, of misunderstood kindness and sacrifice. He endured real temptations. He felt human limitations, and plainly said so. Having accepted the limitations of human life and becoming in a true sense a Son of Man that He might make us sons af God He needed and constantly received the enduement of the Holy Spirit. It was given him without any limit or measure. His Father filled Him and gave Him power, as no prophet of old had ever received illumination. On the mountain of transfiguration the glory seemed almost too great for the flesh. But it must not be forgotten that His experiences under the unparalleled illumination of the Spirit were still in a true sense human; otherwise the real idea of the incarnation is lost, and He could not be a true mediator. We cannot penetrate the mystery of death in the slightest degree, and we must not speak as though we could tell what took place in the death of this unparalleled Personality, but in this gift of Self, atonement is made for us. It is, however, certain that the death of the body in no way ended the LIFE. Christ, the Word of God, has never ceased to be, and He is proved to be the Son of God by the power of His endless Life. It always has been difficult to see how Christ could be both human and Divine, and some over-emphasize one phase of His nature, and some the other, but if we knew all about Divine Nature and human nature, we should see that One Person could in perfect degree express them both to man, and we should also see that Father, Son and Holy Spirit are one God in simple unity from the Divine point of view, but from our human point of view expressed in three forms; as each ray of light is to us light, color and energy, though in perfect, indivisible unity. It in no way affects the continuity of the infinite circle of Divinity that at one arc it breaks out in human form, and shows us the Divine glory in the face of Jesus Christ, and we must not fail, by being perplexed over the mystery of His nature, to let Him bring us to the Father. Some day we shall UNDERSTAND what our deepest faith now tells us is true, that Jesus Christ is in deepest truth Divine.

CHAPTER XXVIII

BEATITUDES IN THE GOSPEL

THERE is a great spiritual law, that it is impossible to get something for nothing. This seems at first to contradict the teaching that "grace is free," that "whosoever will, may come," and that salvation is "without money and without price." But the minute we look below the surface, we find that there is no contradiction here.

In many of our institutions of learning in America "education is free," but that does not mean that education is conferred upon the student without effort and co-operation on his part, or that he can sit with folded hands and "receive" an education. In the same way character is free—i. e., it does not cost a man any money-fee to have a good character; but nevertheless, no man can "receive" a character ready made, or have it supplied to him, without moral effort and a struggle with, and victory over, temptations.

All the beatitudes of the Gospel are of this same nature. In one sense the "blessings" are as free as air and sunshine, but we see at once that they come only when a certain spiritual state, or condition of life, has been realized. In other words, it is impossible to have the wider view until the mountain is climbed, though the view above is just as "free" as it is below, on the ground level. Look at the beatitudes and see how they all illustrate that spiritual law of which we spoke at first.

There is the beatitude of seeing God, but it is granted only to "the pure in heart," which means, of course, that seeing God is the normal result of getting the heart pure; it becomes then "second nature" to see God. God does not confer this beatitude as a free gift. What He does give freely is the opportunity of making the heart pure; and the spiritual eyes open to see God, just as fast as we climb up into the life where such vision is possible. The blessedness comes with the quality of life.

There is again the beatitude of being filled, but it comes only to those who have been feeling the sorrow and emptiness and the pangs of hunger and thirst. It is the passion for righteousness which God blesses, and without the passion, the beatitude which attaches to it cannot be received. There is the beatitude of "having the kingdom of heaven," but there is a spiritual state required first which is called "being poor in spirit." You get the blessing only as you enter the state. "Poor in spirit" does not mean being depressed or despondent, or of no account in the earth; but it does mean coming to the condition where we realize our poverty of soul and our need of God and His riches. It is the sense of incompleteness and worthlessness, followed by the incoming flood of God's completeness and fulness. When God comes, of course the kingdom of heaven comes.

Then, too, there is the beatitude of being "comforted," but it comes only to those who have gone down into the baptism of some hard experience. It is "light after darkness, peace after pain." It is not too much to say, that God never could be fully known or enjoyed by one who had never been in a furnace of trial. Love is never fully revealed, so long as its "course runs smooth." It is when Love comes to comfort that we catch its real heart and meaning. It is when God comes in to heal and bind up our wounds and to fill a great void in our lives that we learn the meaning of this beatitude. Every experience has its own beatitude. At each point on the slopes of Pisgah we get the vision according to our height.

CHAPTER XXIX

WHAT WOULD WE ASK HIM?

IT is interesting and instructive to notice the kind of questions which the disciples and others asked the Master when He was with them in person. They very seldom came to Him to ask about the great central truths. We hear no question about the life of the Spirit, about union with Christ, about the mystery of love and sacrifice, or how to become pure in heart, how to overcome, how to put down all love of sin. They are concerned with times and seasons. When is this new kingdom coming? Are we to sit on exalted seats in the kingdom? Whose sin made this man blind? Ought we to pay tribute to Cæsar? What does He mean by "a little while"? Whose wife shall she be in the resurrection? Why could not we cast the devil out? In what mountain shall we pray? These are some of the familiar questions, and they often break in upon Him when He is unfolding some deep spiritual truth, with a question which shows that their thought was about the husk, while his was concerned with the inner kernel. How often the parent smiles as he listens to the artless questions of the child who is never tired of asking, and whose questions show what the little mind is busy with. So those who gathered round the Lord plied Him with the childish problems which filled their thought, and missed their opportunity to ask Him of the deeper things which our hearts so desire to have unveiled.

But what should we ask Him to-day, if He stood in our streets, or came to eat at our tables? Many of our questions would still be about the husk, and we should still fail to learn those deeper truths of which He had to tell His disciples they were not yet ready to hear. One can imagine the pushing crowd about Him to-day, asking the questions which are uppermost. Shall we sprinkle or immerse? Shall we use fermented or unfermented wine in our communion service? Lord, when art Thou coming a second time? Shall we have pastors or silent meetings? Are those who are eternally punished in sight of the blessed? Is the Bible really an inspired book, and is every word literally true? Is it right for Christians to sing? Can infants go to heaven if they have never been baptized? Shall we employ doctors or shall we be healed by faith? He would undoubtedly look sadly upon us and say: "I have many things to say unto you, but ye cannot bear them now." The questions we ask show better than anything else the height of our lives. An ignorant person can hardly ask intelligent questions, and the wiser a man is the wiser will his questions be. So, too, the more spiritual a man is the more profound and important will his problems be. Paul saw Christ for one blessed moment, and his question concerned his whole career: "What shall I do, Lord?" and the answer came, "I will show thee." He had no curiosity about husks, he wanted to know how to be obedient to his "heavenly vision." The trouble with Christians to-day, wherever there is trouble, is that they have too shallow concerns, their thoughts are on surface matters. They do not plow down to the core and essence of religion and penetrate the crust so that the glowing stream of life may break through. Let us put away childish things and ask for light on the subjects which really concern our soul and our relation to Him who is Life and Love.

CHAPTER XXX

ROBES OF RIGHTEOUSNESS

HARDLY any other word has held a greater place in the spiritual and moral history of our race than righteousness. There are a few words of higher meaning, but righteousness is one of the coinages of the spiritual kingdom of mighty significance. It was the burden of the message of the great Hebrew prophets; it was the keynote of the Forerunner's call to the Jews; it is in the warp and woof of Christ's teaching; it is the very substance of Paul's doctrine, and it is the great principle of Luther's Reformation—"Righteousness by faith."

Therefore, any type of Christianity which has righteousness left out is weak and nerveless, as would be a man without bones or an oak tree without fibres. The very kingdom of heaven itself IS RIGHTEOUSNESS, as the Apostle of righteousness tells us, and the crown which awaits God's true saints is no crown of fading leaves or flowers, but a crown of Righteousness. And yet there is a kind of righteousness which is called "filthy rags," no garment at all, but only patches and tatters, and strangely enough it has been a very popular kind in all the ages. This ragged righteousness is a selfish sort, which men expect to get by their own unaided efforts, and to use solely for their own ends, and for this reason it is properly called self-righteousness. It feeds pride and at the same time hardens the heart. It makes its possessor cold and narrow and loveless. He does right very much as a machine would. If there is any man in the world that needs to be saved it is such a self-centered righteous man, who thanks God he is not like other men, or who boasts like the "elder brother" that he has stayed at home and done his duty. The world is somehow so made that no man can be "self-made," or live unto himself. The self-righteous man is one who boasts that he is morally "self-made;" he owes nothing to anything but his own efforts. Now it is just as impossible for a man to be righteous alone by his own efforts, as it is for a merchant to do business alone. No person begins to be spiritual until he loses himself, until he finds something better than himself to worship and serve, so that the first step for salvation and toward real righteousness is to realize one's insufficiency and incompleteness alone, and to find another CENTRE of life, for there is no salvation possible for a man until his heart goes out beyond himself. As soon as Christ possesses a man, he no longer does right by rule and as a machine. His heart kindles with love, and it is first nature to do right to those he loves. Righteousness is a necessary fruit of love, and the deeper the love the wider the sway of righteousness. If a man loved absolutely, he would become absolutely righteous, for it would become his greatest pain to harm anybody in the universe. Christ's righteousness is, then, not to be sought as an end in itself; it comes with love. It is "put on" as fast as we put on Christ. It is no more a thing of patches and rags; it is a robe which covers the whole man. It is, too, a vital spiritual principle, which links the Christian into union with the interests of all other men, and makes a complete network of relation, and this kind of love-born righteousness is not merely for earthly society; it is as well an essential quality of the kingdom of heaven, and it is a most fitting crown for those who "keep the faith."

CHAPTER XXXI

TWO TYPICAL CONCEPTIONS OF SALVATION

"ARE you saved?" is a question often asked at revival meetings, and often answered in a vague, uncertain way: "I hope so," or "I think I am." "Saved" has always been a great word in Christianity, and most Christians would feel that the power of Christianity was gone if it should lose its message of salvation. We are Christians not because we believe a beautiful philosophical theory, but because we have found a way of salvation, and because in very fact men are "saved."

But it is pretty evident that opinions differ as soon as we ask what is meant by salvation, by being saved, and we find that many persons say they do not know whether they are saved or not, which means, of course, that they do not know what salvation is.

There have been in the history of Christian thought two typical conceptions of salvation. To a certain number of persons "being saved" means being sure of heaven. Salvation is an escape. Sin got into the world through the fault of our first ancestor. It was then entailed upon the race, and the whole family came under the judicial condemnation of the Sovereign. His justice demanded punishment, but His love found a means of escape. Those who accept the Divine plan of escape have their sins covered and the consequences removed, and they are saved by grace. Salvation, according to this thought, is essentially a judicial plan, a method to repair the breach which our fallen nature has made. There are, of course, a great many different ways of expressing this view, and it is held in a very great variety of phases, but at bottom it is essentially judicial.

The other conception is best illustrated by the parable of the Prodigal Son. It considers personal, voluntary sin as the only possible separation between man and God. A man without sin is a child of God. But sin immediately separates, and it puts its own mark upon the sinner. He is unsaved because he is away from God, because he is a servant to sin, and because he has put himself out of Divine relationship. He has gone to the enemy's country and God seems foreign to him, and he is afraid of Him. Sin always produces separation and fear, and any man living in sin is "lost." How can such a man be saved? The only way he can be saved is by finding God and getting free of sin. Jesus Christ expresses God's love, which reaches the most desperate prodigal. He is the Incarnation of God, living among men to show them how the Divine Heart yearns for them to become sons of God, and then suffering and dying to make His love reach all who in any land or in any age hear how He died for them. This mighty love breaks across any separation which man's sin makes and tells every prodigal that he may be a son, for God is a Father.

The essence of the Gospel on the Divine side is this expression of forgiveness and love. The essence of the Gospel on the human side lies in the fact that it turns the face to God and sets free from sin. It makes the man a new man. It makes the slave to sin a free man. It makes the prodigal a son. It does nothing short of transforming a human soul by linking it to its Divine source, and by waking in it the joy and love which belong to life with God. Salvation, according to this thought, is essentially a transformation. It is much more than an escape. It is a present consciousness of Divine possession, and the enjoyment of freedom and sonship. Those who are saved with this kind of salvation know it.

CHAPTER XXXII

PUTTING OFF AND PUTTING ON

TOO many persons want to put on before they put off. They want to dress in white robes before they have disrobed themselves of their filthy rags. They want the new man without losing the old man. They want the angel wings and the flesh-pots too. There is a proverbial expression that certain people "want the earth with a gold fence round it." There are very many of these persons in the church.

It is surely all right to expect large things, to have high aims and wide-reaching purposes, but there are impossible attainments even for Christians, for there are Divine Laws which operate in the realm of the spiritual life, and which must be obeyed. One of these laws is the unalterable truth that the old man and new man cannot live and flourish in the same person. It is impossible for a caterpillar to be both a caterpillar and a butterfly at the same time. It cannot both eat cabbage leaves and suck honey from flowers. There comes a sharp moment in its career when the caterpillar nature ends. The old hulk cracks open and the empty case is left, as the new creature enters upon a new career, with new tastes and desires and loves. It leaves its cabbage plant, for it has found the honeysuckle. It does not miss its numerous legs to crawl with, for it has wings to soar with. Well, this is a parable, as everything in nature really is to those who have eyes to see.

We lose both worlds when we try to get both at the same time. We must choose between rags and robes, between holiness and easy worldliness, between the old man whom we know so well and the new man who "after God is created in righteousness and true holiness." Now, sanctification does not mean pulling a white robe on over the old dress which the world and sin have stained and defiled. It is both destructive and constructive. It begins with the sloughing off of the old. It comes with fan and fire. It winnows and burns. But this is only that there may be a genuine constructive work. No saint is made by the putting off process alone. It would be like trying to make a butterfly by cutting off the legs of a caterpillar. A process of life must split the old hulk and work a recreation. The destruction of the old and the putting on of the new is a part of the same Divine process. We often wish we might know beforehand of God's resurrection power. It seems such a far-off and miraculous thing! Well, we may know about it. It is just the marvelous thing about our Christianity that every one of us may now have an experience of the working of the mighty power which raised Christ from the dead and set Him in the Heavenlies (Eph. 1 : 19, 20). The power of His resurrection is revealed when a new man is created and an old man is put off.

CHAPTER XXXIII

TO WHOM SHALL WE GO?

PAUL could say in his ringing words, "Neither life nor death can separate me from the love of God in Christ Jesus." Strangely enough the life test is much harder to stand than the death test. Most converts in the power of their new-found Lord would stand like a rock if they had to face death for their faith. They would say with Peter, who could not face a simple maiden's question, "I will die for thee." But then comes the daily life. Neighbors are mean and hateful. Every day has its vexatious trials. The fervor of the first consecration wanes. Christians themselves prove to be imperfect and their profession runs ahead of their practice. Those who used to speak encouraging words are now silent, and one feels that nobody cares whether he goes ahead or slips back. Hot impulses come and do not get checked. The narrow way seems hard and the old life looks more attractive. So the slipping goes on step by step, and generally without any willful turning

of the back the feet have drifted into the old
path again and the "possible saint" has become an actual sinner. Sometimes it is the
man's own fault that his lamp burns low, but
probably more often it is the fault of other
Christians. We are our brothers' keepers and
they need endless patience and help and over-
sight until they are rooted and grounded
themselves. The sheep in the great parable
represents the sinner who drifts away step by
step without intending really to leave the fold.
The sheep feeds away and suddenly realizes
that it is out of the pasture and lost. It was
one out of a hundred. The lost coin represents the sinner who gets lost through somebody's carelessness. It is no fault of the coin
that it lies hidden in the dirt in the dark corner of the room instead of being found on the
cord round the brow of the wife, as the Eastern
custom is. Here the proportion is one out of
ten. It is a sad fact in our Christianity that
we cannot keep all we win, that our deserters
are so numerous, and that such a multitude of
people straggle along half way between both
camps and own no hearty allegiance to either.
Much of this trouble is due to the fact that
they never really were "joined to the Lord,"
to use the beautiful apostolic phrase. They
never actually found the pearl. They saw

their Lord a long way off and felt a joyous rapture at the sight, but never drew any nearer to Him. They never honestly faced the situation and decided to "lose themselves to find themselves." It is only those who have dwelt with Him who can say "To whom shall we go?" when He asks if they expect to leave Him. Some Christians teach a doctrine which they call "once in grace always in grace." It is hard to tell just what they mean by it, but if they mean that one who is really born again can never go back afterwards, we do not agree with their position, nor do we find any support for such teaching. But we do believe that the most of those who go back do so because they never really went far enough to find the jewel. They are like the gold seekers who never go over the Skaguay Pass and when they come from Alaska they bring no Klondike gold dust with them, for all the gold dust is on the other side of the pass!

CHAPTER XXXIV

THE RAREST HUMAN QUALITY

MUCH has been written to show how love is the greatest thing in the world, but there is one human quality much more rare than love—we mean SYMPATHY. It is not difficult for human beings to love, for we all love the lovable when we see it. " We needs must love the highest when we see it." Then, too, love has a sure reward. Love is almost never one-sided. We love because we are loved. It is a mutual, reciprocal quality. It is a kind of spiritual double-entry, in which the sides balance. It is give and receive. There is no state or experience so rapturous and joyous as that of loving. It is second nature to love, and almost nobody gets through life without having loved sometime, on a higher or lower level. But sympathy is a very different thing. One has to be almost angelic to sympathize. It is possible for selfish persons to love, but it is not possible for them to feel genuine sympathy. It is an absolutely unselfish quality. Most persons think they are sympathizing when they are not at all. They see some one in trouble, and they say with a sad, solemn tone, "Poor fellow, I am very sorry for you, you have my hearty sympathy," and they go to their house "justified," but down deep in their hearts they were rejoicing all the time that they were not like that "poor fellow," and they were exulting in their happier fortune. That is not sympathy. Another class of persons say nothing to the one in trouble, because they do not know what to say. They act awkward and restrained when they are with him, but try hard all the time to be natural and easy, and to talk of everything else but his trouble, so as not to hurt his feeling or stir his deeps. Still other persons avoid those who are in trouble, and say in hushed voices to their neighbors, "Poor So and So is having a hard time, isn't he?" Of course this is not sympathy. The result is that a person in deep trouble in this world feels pretty much alone, and when he finds real sympathy he is as surprised as a desert traveler is when he finds a beautiful flower, and he is sure it must have had a divine origin.

Some of the most beautiful passages of the Gospel tell of Christ's sympathy. Like the transfiguration, they show us at once the divine nature which was in Him, and no human title more truly glorifies Him than that of the "Great Sympathizer." He shared the troubles and sadness of others, and this is the essential element of sympathy. The word means "feeling or suffering with." The easy, well-meant words of pity are like a cold crust thrown as alms. One genuine pulse of fellow feeling, a true sharing of the burden of the heart are worth more than a million words of sentiment. But alas, that other is so hard to realize, is so rare, is so divine. It is the one lone flower which we hardly know except as a pressed specimen between the leaves of a book. Those who give it are most like Christ of all human beings.

CHAPTER XXXV

NOT CUNNINGLY DEVISED FABLES

WE have no difficulty in putting our faith in things which we know are REAL, and the moment we establish the reality of any fact, it at once affects our actions accordingly. Nobody starts for the Klondike until he has evidence which convinces him that the coveted yellow dust is really there. But as soon as the reality is established the gold seeker forgets every obstacle and acts upon his belief. People laughed at the theory of Columbus until he gave convincing evidence of its reality, and then ship after ship was pointed toward the west and the new world became as definite a country as the old world. The Church tried to make Galileo take back his statement that the earth moves, but as soon as the fact was clearly established everybody adopted the idea, and now a man would be thought insane if he should maintain that the earth had no motion. So we might go on with illustrations, but it is clear to everybody that the world believes in a thing as soon as its reality is established, and this belief immediately affects action.

Now, why are not more people genuinely religious? Why do so few persons seek FIRST the kingdom of God? It is because they are not certain of the reality of unseen things. The trouble with all half-hearted, compromising Christians, is that something else is much more real to them than God is. They look at the things that are seen and they find them real; they look at the things which are not seen and they are not quite sure whether they are real or not; and the result is that they seek first the things they are sure of. All who are honest with themselves will agree with us that this is just their difficulty.

Now, the transcendent thing about Christianity is this, that for those who are willing to see, it establishes the reality of God and makes His kingdom one of the surest facts in the world. God is no longer an "unknown God." We are not left blindly to guess about Him and His will and nature. He has dwelt among us. This is the Christian message! The Sun has risen and we have seen its light. The curtain is forever pulled back from before the mercy-seat, and we know the reality of the love of God. It is as much a fact as the orbit of the moon is. The kingdom of God is no longer a dream of poets or a vision of seers. The most matter-of-fact man may see the kingdom of God extending its sway. It is present wherever in the name of Christ a man overcomes sin and becomes holy and righteous. Wherever darkness and evil are driven back, and light and truth conquer, wherever saintly, Christlike lives are made out of weak, tempted, sin-stained human beings; wherever souls are renewed and transformed, there the reality of the King and of the kingdom is established.

The Incarnation of God in Christ, and the unmistakable spread of His kingdom, are two central facts. A person's first business in life should be to grasp their reality. No man can live an easy, compromising life after he has established the reality of these two facts. Let him see the light of the knowledge of the glory of God in the face of Jesus Christ, and let him realize that the grain of mustard seed is really growing into a mighty tree, which is filling the earth, and his whole life will be lifted to a higher plane of living.

CHAPTER XXXVI

SABBATH OBSERVANCE

THE observance of the Sabbath is older than the records of history, and it is now certain that the setting apart of one day in seven did not originate with the promulgation of the Mosaic law, but that law simply gave emphasis and definiteness to an old, time-honored custom, and the book of Genesis significantly traces its origin back to a day of rest after six creative days " in the beginning." The Puritans made a stern effort to re-establish a "holy day," a day of rest, a day of solemnity, on which all the wheels of toil should cease and all gaiety and jollity be forgotten. They were partially successful, though they never reached the complete standstill which characterized a Jewish Sabbath, where stoning was the penalty for picking up sticks for a fire, and the carrying of a rug-couch was a dreadful offense. The reaction from the Puritan Sabbath has carried us far toward the other extreme, and it has become a serious question with all earnest Christians how properly to keep the Sabbath holy.

We may as well recognize at once that the old Jewish Sabbath can no more be restored than can the practice of circumcision, and the early Christians certainly looked upon the Jewish Sabbath, as kept in their day, as a part of the intolerable bondage of the old system. In fact, Paul speaks clearly against its legalistic observance, and the early church swept it forever away with the other ceremonials of the law which Christ's cross nullified.

But the infant church from its first beginning took one day out of the seven and called it the Lord's Day. It was the First-day of the week, the day forever glorified and consecrated by the Resurrection of the Christ, who thus proved himself the Son of God with power and the true Head of the church. This "Lord's Day" is our Christian holy day, and its true observance must be determined in the light of Christ's revelation. It is not meant for bondage but for freedom. It is set apart and consecrated to man's highest uses. No man can be at his best if he slavishly toils seven days in a week and has no period to rest his body and to commune with his God. That is a way to make life brutish. The whole world needs a time of hush. The rush and turmoil, the grind of labor, and the search for enjoyment, the clink of wine glasses and the indulgence in dangerous pleasures—with no break or interruption—would leave man a distorted wreck. Upon every life under the blue sky the peace and quiet of the Lord's Day should fall and let the reality of higher things impress itself. Spiritual life demands one day at least in seven, and no people can remain long spiritual if the world gets every day.

This holy day is necessary for preserving the sweet influences of the home circle; the hard pressed laborer must have it unless he is to be made a blind machine with no higher, sweeter life. Around this Lord's Day a circle of separation should be drawn. We must not let it become like other days. It should be to our souls what the spring showers are to the flowers, and we should make it a Lord's Day to all who are weary and heavy-laden. It is to save life, not to destroy. It is to lift hearts into an ampler and diviner life. It is to make earth a holier place, and though we cast no stone at him who picks up sticks on this day, as in the old dispensation, yet it is our sacred duty to make it a day of holy uses for the higher life.

CHAPTER XXXVII

THE GOSPEL OF THE SON OF GOD

SOLDIERS are always talking about the enormous "waste" of powder which is a feature of every battle whether on land or sea. For every bullet that takes effect hundreds are shot into the air or into the ground. If this were not so an attacking army would be annihilated before it reached the position it is attempting to carry. The wildness of the aim is therefore one of the merciful features of a battle.

Strangely enough this wildness of aim, this same waste of ammunition, characterizes all our great spiritual contests as well. In the hot and prolonged fight with the forces of sin nothing is more discouraging than this same false aim and waste of energy. Read the history of our nineteen centuries of Christianity and see how few of the shots have been straight at the enemy's head. Look at the militant church to-day and see what a tremendous waste of force there is. Christians seem bound to fight everything but the real enemy, and when they find a man who does open fire on the central fortress, the others are quite likely to open fire on him, because he isn't shooting nine-tenths of his weapons into the air.

Jesus Christ always refused the random aims and went straight to the mark. The air-shooters of His day were always trying to turn Him off the main line to an attack on phantom enemies, but He never swerved an iota. They came with their metaphysical question, whether hereditary sin made a poor man blind, or whether it was his own sin. Christ brushed away the whole logical quibble and showed them that the main thing was the present opportunity to work the work of God on the man who needed help. They never ceased to buzz about Him with hard problems about the Messianic kingdom. He refused to waste force on idle discussion with those who were too blind in their own conceits to appreciate any new truth, and He simply announced that "the pure in heart see God," and the poor in spirit are in the kingdom. Tricky questions about the resurrection and tribute money were simply occasions for Him to unfold the great truth that God is the God of the living, whether in the visible or invisible world, and that we can safely trust Him, and that neither is to be slighted.

It is easy for us to get over our depth on every subject connected with spiritual things if we only allow ourselves to tumble into the slough of speculation. But what is gained by it? Religion wants to keep out of all these quicksands and deal with facts that can be tested.

The Gospel of the Son of God is the message for to-day as it was when the "blessed feet" trod the hills of Judea. Tell men as He did of the Father's love. Declare everywhere His power and His readiness to forgive sin. Show as He did that the pure heart has an immediate evidence, an unmistakable proof of God. Herald the kingdom of God as a fact, and make men see its reality. Preach the Gospel of Redemption—Christ giving His life for sinners and in infinite love showing how the Divine Heart yearns for every soul. Make men understand that Christianity is not a web of metaphysical and abstract theories, but God revealing Himself in a Son and so giving Life to the world. Oh, friends, the Gospel of the Son is too precious a truth to be wasted in sham battles. Let us present it straight to men's hearts.

CHAPTER XXXVIII

A FAITH THAT HONORS GOD

ONE of the most striking characteristics of the great Hebrew prophets was their steady faith that God was at work in the world and that His truth and righteousness would triumph. They looked at the dark foregrounds of their own time and clearly saw the shadows, but they refused to conclude that this was all of the picture. In calm faith they all saw a light breaking over the hills in the background and they declared that the dawn, the morning star, the faint light, held the promise of a full, bright day to be.

This steady faith in God, in even fuller degree, characterized the Apostle Paul. No heaped up total of evils ever swerved him from his belief in ultimate victory. The bigotry of the Jews, the fickleness of the Galatians, the idolatry of Athens, the corruption and immorality of Corinth, the brutality and sin of Rome, the hardships of his own life, never for a moment clouded for him the heavenly vision. Hear him say, "All things work

A FAITH THAT HONORS GOD

together for good to them that love God." "If God be for us, who can be against us?" "The whole creation is groaning and travailing, waiting for the manifestation of the sons of God." And the author of the Epistle to the Hebrews shows the same heroic faith. "We see not yet all things put under His feet, but we see Jesus." A more modern Christian, living in a period of turmoil and strife and when spiritual religion had few voices, showed his spiritual kinship with God's faithful of earlier times in these beautiful words of hope: "I saw an ocean of darkness and death, but I saw an INFINITE ocean of life and light flow over the ocean of darkness and death. And in this I saw the goodness of God." *

Too many Christians to-day, lack this prophetic and apostolic faith. They deliver hopeless Jeremiads over the condition of things. They are pessimists through and through. They see only the dark foreground, with no rising sun lighting up the hills of the background. They are very sure of heaven, it may be, but they have no faith that God can do anything for this poor wreck of a world. They are afraid that the Bible is going to lose its place of influence. They are afraid Christ is going to lose His divine authority. They fear God

* George Fox's "Journal,"

is going to lose the glory of being Creator. Those who take this gloomy view need to go to Horeb and hear "the still, small voice" again. There is no place for a pessimistic Christianity. It sounds too much like the despair of the men on the way to Emmaus: "We trusted that it had been he which should have redeemed Israel," but now He is crucified and the hope is gone! All such dark outlooks and despairing views grow out of a faith which really dishonors God. It implies that God is "asleep, or, peradventure, He taketh a journey;" at any rate He is absent and is not busied in the events of our world. We need to get back to the earlier, truer faith in God. Not a sparrow falls, not a lily is made without His care. Does He, peradventure, care less for America than for Israel? Does He make revelations in one age and let it all go for naught in a later age? Does He give His son to redeem the world and then let the Redemption become outdated and ineffective? Impossible! He is the God of the living. He is with us to-day. His victories are sure. He is making saints now. His kingdom is coming. "He is working all things up to better," as Clement used to say. All things work for good under His hand. Christ has risen, the Spirit is with us.

CHAPTER XXXIX

WHAT MIGHT HAVE BEEN, BUT IS NOT

THE ancient Romans used to say that even God himself cannot undo what has been done. How often we see too late that we might have made our life and our world entirely different if we had only known, but now the opportunity has gone! These too-late discoveries, our useless hindsights where we needed foresights, are among the hardest experiences of life. If we could only go back over our steps and make our choice over again, how different the outcome would be. But in this world of ours this can never be done. The decision of a moment determines a whole lifetime, and no amount of sorrow or wishing turns the shadow back on the dial. How stubborn and unyielding the laws of the universe seem, and the change of one little circumstance would make us so happy! But just that "little circumstance" cannot be changed after it has come to pass, and our lives must flow in different channels accordingly.

A very slight "water-shed" determines sometimes the course of the rivers of a continent; a child's foot on a tender sappling has caused the twist which mars the oak of a hundred years' growth; and that one deed which we cannot undo has made the curve in the direction of our human life. The lost opportunity comes not back to us, the spilled milk on the ground flows not back into our pail, the missed train does not come back to take us on. Well, is this a blind, hard fate, or is it the will of a loving Father? The ancients called it Fate. We see in it a sure token of love. How could we learn the lessons of life, how could we become men and women of character, if our deeds brought no sure consequences, and if the past could be undone at a wish? Is that mother kind and loving who changes her will to suit every wish of her child? No, the kindest mother teaches her child the meaning of consequences, and she trains the child to make good choices by showing the inexorable result of bad choices. So God deals with us. His main purpose in his "dealings" is to make men of good will. He does not want fickle, unstable men with wills as variable as the wind. But if life had no stubborn and unyielding laws, if we could at will retrace our steps and gather up our lost opportunities and try over again as soon as we began to feel any uncomfortable consequences we should never attain the measure of manhood. The product would be a jelly-fish type of man with no stamina. The child must learn that fire will burn, the traveler must find out that trains do not wait for his convenience, and we must all gain the experience that life is made beautiful and successful not by late hindsights, but by wise foresights.

Even in these hard and trying "consequences" of life God is thinking only of our good, and in our sad and bitter "might have beens" He teaches us how to achieve the "may bes" of the future.

CHAPTER XL

THE PEACE OF GOD

"THE Peace of God" is used in two senses —as the Peace which PERVADES the Divine nature and the Peace which He GIVES. We sometimes wonder, with our narrow vision, how a Being who sees all the wrongs, all the sins, all the blunders, all the struggles and failures of the world, can have Peace. If our human eyes could run to and fro through all the earth and see all its miseries, would it not distract us and drive all Peace from our mind? But the infinite Mind sees the goal of all things, knows that it is all working together for good, foresees the ripe fruit where we see only bud, and to His ear the myriad sounds of the universe make a perfect harmony where we, in our narrow range, hear jarrings and discords. He who saw more deeply into life than any other soul who has ever walked the earth, who felt the harsh and tuneless jangle of lives out of harmony with God, and who knew the glory of life attuned to the Divine Will, talked much of His Peace. His great desire for His followers was that they might have His Peace, and He promised to "give" His Peace to them. Now here is one of the miracles of Christianity that a human heart in the midst of afflictions and trials and misunderstandings may have the "Peace of God." But it can come only with surrender. When a human will runs at an angle with the Divine Will and refuses to go parallel with that will, when it refuses to accept the terms and conditions of God, Peace is impossible. Most of us are like the little child who resists and fails to see the father's good purpose, who storms and cries and kicks instead of accepting the father's will and trusting his goodness. As soon as the child learns and says: "I will, dear father," a peace comes which was impossible while it maintained its own will against the father's. Beyond all understanding is the Peace which comes when a soul learns the Father's good purpose and accepts it joyfully, without resistance or reserve. The surface-life, like the surface of the ocean, is heaving and restless, it is at the mercy of every breeze and every storm-cloud. There are hours of sunshine, moments of joy, yet no true Peace. But enter deeper into the life of God, as the diver does into the ocean, and there is Peace. It is the

Peace of God. It is not a life of dead calm, of sluggish inaction. There are onward moving currents, but the storms and turmoil of the surface are felt no more. At the heart of things there is Peace. Peace is declared! There is no hostility on the Divine side, and yet we do not accept the terms unconditionally, we do not have the Peace of God. The jangle of our lives grates upon us and jars upon the ears of our neighbors. The harmony will not come. Over our restless, ruffled lives the Master of the Galilean lake says: "Peace, My Peace I give unto you."

CHAPTER XLI

IS TRUE RELIGION EMOTIONAL?

THERE is no part of man so little understood as what we generally call his "emotional nature." Why, under certain circumstances, should the lip quiver and the tears flow, and under other circumstances the heart beat high, the eyes flash, the cheeks color? Nobody, in the midst of an emotion, ever stops to investigate his feeling, but even if he did he would find that it was indescribable. The most noticeable thing about it is the plain fact that the body is MOVED, generally the heart is affected, and almost always the face reveals the mental state.

Now, is religion intellectual, or is it emotional? Does it consist in believing certain truths and understanding and accepting certain facts, or is it rather an intense feeling of love and adoration, a heart moved with a sense of God's grace and mercy, which expresses itself in the face, a rapturous emotion which swells through the whole being? Some persons take one view and some the other.

There are Christians whose religion is a calm, cold and bloodless belief, which moves them no more than their belief that Columbus discovered America. They are shocked at every sign of emotion. They are able to set forth logically the whole plan of salvation and to distinguish clearly between what is orthodox and what is unsound, but they would stand *unmoved* before the holy of holies and the wings of the cherubim. There are, on the other hand, Christians who would not call this religion at all. For them religion begins and ends in emotion. They do not want "intellectual preaching;" they want heart preaching. They like meeting where the tide rises high, and they estimate the spiritual worth of a meeting by the amount of enthusiasm and intensity manifested. Frequently they tremble with feeling, and it is hard not to shout or in some way give vent to the overflowings of the heart. This type of Christian reaches the climax, as everybody knows, in the negro revival, but he is found in some degree in almost every church. It seems to us that there is very little choice between these two extreme views, for they seem to us both wrong.

True religion is neither coldly intellectual or purely emotional. It consists of correct belief, an apprehension of God's truth, and an intense love and devotion, a profound appreciation of His forgiveness and unbounded love. Leave out either element and the religion is warped and one-sided. There must be a heavenly vision, a revelation in the knowledge of Him, a fixed idea which runs through the life and steadies it, but with this there must be also a heart full to overflowing which throbs out its "Praise God." A religion with this heart side, this love part left out, is like a brookless desert. It would be much like a family in which each member shows intelligent respect for the others, but no warm, beating love.

Yes, religion must have genuine emotion. But there is no part of our nature so hard to control and keep balanced as the emotions. Children have no control over their emotion, and a good part of the education of life lies in the direction and control of emotion and passion. The earlier love is demonstrative and passionate; the later, deeper love is calm and mighty. A religion that runs into excessive emotion often gets but slight hold of the inner being, of the man, and it not seldom fails to keep him firm in the hour of test. It evaporates after the emotional excitement is over. But the man of spiritual power is one who clearly sees the truth and is established in it, and at the same time feels that calm and mighty throb of love, which grows out of personal experience of God's unspeakable gift, and who directs this vision of truth and this emotion of love and joy to the making of a noble, beautiful and holy life.

CHAPTER XLII

THE DOWNWARD PRESSURE

THERE is a pressure of fifteen pounds weight on every square inch of our bodies, caused by the weight of the column of air which reaches from us perhaps fifty miles up into space. Every one of us carries day after day this enormous load of air. Multiply the number of square inches on the surface of the body by fifteen, and you have the number of pounds. It gives a novel sensation when we stop to think that we are bearing on our head and shoulders a tower of air taller than the highest mountain, rising into a cold and lonely region which no living thing has ever penetrated. And yet we never feel this pressure, and it does not weigh us down or hinder our work, because there is an upward pressure equal to the downward, a pressure from within equal to that from without. In other words the pressures are perfectly balanced so that we are buoyed up as much as we are weighed down.

There is something beautiful in this balance of pressure, and it is this which really makes life possible. Some of us have discovered that this balance of pressures is not confined to the material world; there is something very much like it in spiritual experience. Nobody gets very far on in life without feeling a tremendous pressure from without,—the burdens, and cares,—the world's great load which settles on us, and almost threatens to crush the life down. It does break the spirit of many a poor fellow, and he goes to wreck under it.

The only way to find relief is to over-balance this weight by a contrary pressure which buoys up the life, and enables one to go steadily on without being crushed by the weary weight. This overcoming force, this buoying power is indispensable for all true living. It does not take away the loads or the burdens or the trials, but it enables a "heavy laden" soul to find rest in the midst of struggle, for the buoying power overcomes the weight. Emerson's advice has long been a proverb: "Hitch your wagon to a star." That is good advice for those rare souls who hardly live on the earth anyway, and who are not freighted and weighted with such a load of real difficulties that the stars seem too far away to be harnessed to with success. But most of us want to feel that a tender, loving Person is close within our reach, that He shares our load, and gives us an easy yoke, that a union with Him brings with it the overcoming force which more than balances the pressure. Every living thing that grows rises upward in spite of the force of gravitation, and overcomes its "law." The law of life has dominion over this law of weight, and the tiny hare-bell pushes up toward the sun by the force of the life within itself. So also the law of the spirit of life in Christ Jesus makes a soul free from all downward pressures, and enables him to carry his loads as easily as he bears the high column of air.

If one goes up even two thousand feet on a mountain, the downward pressure is less, and the air grows much rarer. Breathing is quickened, the pulse beats faster, the cheeks grow redder, and the bodily temperature becomes higher. Life in high altitudes has a vigor which is strange to the lower levels. It is possible, too, to live a spiritual life on a high level, to overcome the stagnation and low pulse and half-vigor, and to rise, like God's sky-lark, into an ampler air, until that triumphant note breaks out of the full heart, "Thanks be unto God who giveth us the victory through our Lord Jesus Christ!"

CHAPTER XLIII

DOES GOD REALLY LOVE US?

THE main message of the Gospel is the Love of God to men. The proclamation of this Love has always characterized genuine Christianity in every age and in every country. Nobody who rests his faith on the New Testament revelation can doubt the fact of God's Love. But there come times in the personal experience of many when this early faith in God's Love and Goodness is severely tried, when they find themselves clinging in the dark to a single spar, while the billows of doubt break over them. Such times perhaps never come in prosperity. It seems very easy to believe in God's Love when He is giving us just what we want, when all our prayers are answered as soon as we ask.

But when the heavens are as brass and the earth bars of iron, when some hard trial settles over us and we pray and plead for relief and none comes, when the plowshare resistly tears down to our primitive rock and our cries and groans prove ineffectual, then it is that the sensitive heart finds it hard to go on with the happy faith in God's Love. "If He loves me, why does He not help me? If He cares for me why does He not ease me of this too heavy burden?" Such words sometimes almost force themselves to the lips, when "He answers not a word." Those who have had no taste of this hard experience can hardly understand the feeling, and they very naturally take the position which Job's "comforters" did, but many a heart knows what it means to stretch lame hands of faith.

Is there any way to help such perplexed souls who are struggling to keep their faith in the furnace of trial, when no rift seems to open in the brazen sky? The first step must be to show that God's Love is not to be measured by the amount of temporal prosperity and comfort which He bestows, nor would it be an evidence of His Goodness if He always gave just what we want. Such treatment would make "spoiled children," not saints! We must strive, too, to help our perplexed friends see the supreme importance of the spiritual over the temporal. While in our short-sightedness we clutch after things which would give us temporary joy and comfort, God is training us to look only at the things which are unseen and eternal. His method of training often seems like a hard one, but no other method would succeed in weaning us from the things of sense and in preparing us for the enjoyment of spiritual things. Finally we must help our perplexed friends to interpret their lives in the light of Christ's life. His life is the supreme revelation of God's Love and yet His Father never once relieved Him of a hard cup or of a baptism of trial. "If it is possible let this cup pass" is immediately followed by the words, "Thy will be done." The cry, "My God, my God, why hast thou forsaken me?" gives place at once to the calm and trustful words, "Father, into thy hands I commend my spirit." The whole mystery seems solved in that remarkable sentence, "It *became* Him in bringing many sons to glory to make the Captain of their salvation perfect through suffering." If we suppose God has no ultimate purposes in view for us, then of course the hard dispensations would indicate that He did not love us or care for us, but as soon as we look beyond the moment and see His purpose, we can join the chorus: "All things work together for good to them that love God!"

CHAPTER XLIV

THE INCARNATION
'The time draws near the birth of Christ.'

MEN in all ages have longed for a REVELATION, for it has proved a baffling and hopeless struggle to climb up to God, and to find out God by human searching. Plato spoke for all the ancient searchers after truth when he said, "We shall never find the complete truth until God or some God-sent person *comes to us.*" The glory of Christianity is its message that God has come to us. This is the central fact which gives Christianity its overcoming power, and it is this fact of the Incarnation which opens for man the door to life, truth, salvation and spiritual victory.

The moment we make the Incarnation a metaphysical puzzle, the moment we drift out into a sea of speculation about the Trinity, we lose the mighty significance of the fact. The New Testament nowhere treats it as a puzzle or a problem. It simply announces the crowning fact that God tabernacled with men, and manifested His Grace and Glory, and it sets forth the end and purpose of this Divine showing—that we also may become sons. God comes to us that we may come to Him. The Word was with God; the Word was with man, and man with God completes the circle. "I am come, that they might have life," sums up the whole purpose of the Incarnation.

It can never be reduced to a cold and logical doctrine; it must never be pressed as a dead flower and put away in a collection of abstract theological definitions. Let us keep it warm and vital, the perfect blossom whose fragrance still comes as fresh and full of healing as when it broke into flower under the "Syrian blue." "God with us" is the first half of the great message; "we with God" is the second half, and no one fully comprehends the first half until he experiences the second half as a fact in his own life. He who comes to live his life in God no longer wonders and puzzles over the problem, How could God come to us? He realizes that perfected humanity and Divinity are not alien terms. The Divine nature can express itself in a perfect human life. God does not cease to be omnipresent and omniscient, though He at a definite period shows forth His glory and love in a Person who walks among men and teaches with human lips, who loves and suffers, who blesses and heals, who forever makes love and sacrifice and sympathy, and grace and gentleness the supreme realities.

In no other way could God speak to us, and make His revelation comprehensible. If He wrote His thoughts on the vault of the sky we could not understand or interpret them. We must have some one, to reveal Him fully, who understands Him and us, and who speaks in terms common to both, one who completely closes the gap, one who brings God to us and us to God. "He became flesh and dwelt among us." "As many as received Him, to them gave He power to become the sons of God." These two sentences complete the circuit. The Incarnation is a twofold revelation,— a revelation of God and a revelation of human nature, a manifestation of what God is, and a revelation of what man is to be when he comes to God. We know well enough of ourselves what we are, away from Him; the Incarnation reveals what is the hope of our calling, and what the riches of the glory of God's inheritance in us!

CHAPTER XLV

A RELIGION OF FOUR ANCHORS

IN the midst of the racking storm on the Adrian waters, in the darkness of the night, the captain of Paul's vessel cast out four anchors, and waited for the day. It may be only a fanciful symbol, but Paul's words on the ship indicate that he, too, had put out four anchors, which steadied him, and gave him his SPIRITUAL SOLIDITY amid the storms of his life. "I believe God;" "His I am;" "Him I serve;" "God hath given me those who sail with me." This is what we have called a religion of four anchors, and the person who has those four cables out can calmly wait for the day to break.

All religious life and power of high quality spring from a faith which believes God. The old-time strength—the quality in Peter which makes Christ call him the rock-man—comes not from a verbal faith, from a belief in second-hand testimony of any sort, or from "flesh and blood," but from a personal acquaintance with God, and an experimental certainty of

Him. The persons who are really anchored are the ones who reach up through all the lower stages of belief and reliance, and rest unshaken in a faith which goes behind the vail—"I believe God." That is the first step in the making of a spiritual "rock-man."

The second anchor is hardly less important, and that is, the sense of possession—"His I am." Our Quaker poet was expressing this sense when he said:

> "I know not where God's islands lift
> Their fronded palms in air,
> I only know I cannot drift
> Beyond His love and care."

What a life a man might live if he could walk the earth possessed of the unfailing conviction, "I am God's!" It is not simply that he cares for me, nor even alone that He loves me, but "I belong to Him"—that sense of relationship ought to make a Christian as different from ordinary men as a Prince is different from a peasant, for it puts him at once into the rank of nobility, and makes it incumbent upon him to live as a son, not as a hired servant. This consciousness of the divine possession is surely the second step in the making of a spiritual "rock-man."

Then out of our belief of God, and our sense of belonging to Him comes the beautiful certainty that He trusts *us* and gives us His work to do—"whom I serve." Many persons never get grounded in religious experience because they never attain to this certainty that God trusts them and makes them co-workers with Him. Hardly anything strengthens one's life, and solidifies one's faith like active service of some sort. "Backsliders" are generally those who never got to the point of being girded for service, and so never realized how necessary they were to God. It is very significant that after Christ told Peter that he was rock-like, he added also, "I will give unto thee the keys," for the keys in Oriental countries, were the the badge of a trusted servant. Our fourth cable of spiritual strength is the realization that our personal faith is not confined in its effects to the narrow circle of our own lives, but that it has a wonderful influence over the destinies of others—"God has given thee those who sail with thee." No man of faith can live unto himself. The mother's faith affects the destiny of her child; the saint in the neighborhood "affects" the neighbors as though holiness were contagious. Much of the power of singularly spiritual men and women comes from their realization that the destiny of other lives is in some measure upon *them*. This sends the missionary and the slum-worker to their task; this kindles the zeal of the reformer and the prophet, and this is no slight element of strength in the religious life of every profoundly spiritual man. I believe God, I am God's, God trusts and uses me, and I am responsible for others,—these are four anchors, and they are four strands of faith which make solid spiritual character.

CHAPTER XLVI

PRACTICAL HOLINESS

GOD never does things by halves. His purpose is to carry all His work to completion. This is true in the natural world, and it is no less true in the spiritual world. God did not undertake the redemption of man to leave him after all a sin-loving, fluctuating, irritable Christian. He meant him to become a sin-hating, immovable, sweet-natured, positive, spirit-filled man, ready for Life with all its demands and perplexities.

It is too much the custom of easy-going Christians to postpone to the world beyond the triumph over sin, and the OVERCOMING LIFE. It is no glory to anybody to be an overcomer, when there is nothing to be overcome. THIS is the proper sphere for the victory to be won. Right here in the face of the enemy, with all the forces arrayed for a real Armageddon contest, is the opportunity for the strenuous effort to put down sin and to win the victory.

But, as we are so often told, no spiritual victory can be won except through spiritual forces. The more a man glories in his own strength the weaker he is, for alone he is only an atom against powers that attack him at every point, but when he becomes one with Christ through the Spirit he has all the forces of the universe with him. Hold a straw parallel to the current, and the waters of the Gulf Stream will flow through it; hold it across the current, and it is broken to pieces. The first step toward spiritual victory is union and parallelism with the Divine Currents.

Holiness is, then, something real. It is the triumphant Life. It is not a theory or a scheme or a creed. When we find such a Life we go to work to explain how such a life is possible, and we have our theory of it, but the holy Life itself is the real thing, and it is the only thing that can convince the world of the truth of the theory.

Holiness which is not real and practical, is not holiness, any more than sickness is health.

What does practical holiness mean? It means that the man is SAVED FROM SIN; that his life is centred and controlled; that he has the power of the Spirit, and that it makes his daily life victorious. He is not necessarily ecstatic; he may be the calmest man in the town, but he knows the secret of life, and he makes his life correspond with his message.

He ceases to slander or even criticize his neighbors; his only business is to show them the Christ-centered life. He has learned not to call down fire from heaven upon those who do not agree with him, for it does not concern him whether others agree with him or not. That is not his affair, but he is bound to prove that he is in full agreement with the will of God, and that he has the Christ spirit. By that he is tested. He is a good neighbor; he is a good family man; he is a good man to work with in the Church; he seeketh not his own; is not puffed up; doth not behave himself unseemly. All who know him say, Would to God there were ten thousand such. But some will say, Does anybody live such a life; is not all this imagination? Yes, such lives are lived, and such a life is possible for everyone. GOD NEVER DOES ANYTHING BY HALVES. No man can live such a life alone, but God can bring any man into such a life, and it is for this that He redeems us.

CHAPTER XLVII

APPLIED CHRISTIANITY AND WHAT IT SEEKS

IT never does for any church to content itself with setting forth the theory of Christianity. That would be very much like saying to the hungry man, "Be warmed and filled," without opening the cupboard or storehouse. The great function of the church is to illustrate *applied* Christianity.

No one would think of studying the theory of electricity, or physics, or mathematics, without going on to a further practical study of applied electricity, or physics, or mathematics. It is for the sake of the latter that we study the former.

Who would have confidence in the doctor who should devote his whole time to dissecting dead bodies and to the critical study of the structure and parts of the body? We go to the man who has learned by successful experience how to restore health and defeat disease.

The church holds a position of power in the world only in proportion as it applies the

Christianity it teaches in theory, and if it does not succeed in the practical service, something is wrong with its theory.

As advocates and exponents of primitive Christianity revived, it especially becomes us to be sensitive to the needs of those who are "out of Christ," to use that forcible expression of the early church. We cannot possibly remain unconcerned about those who are in this condition, without forfeiting our claim to be members of the body of Christ, for He knew nothing about a religion which did not *save men*. This purpose is the *alpha* and *omega* of His mission.

But the church has suffered loss in every age because of a too superficial conception of salvation. Whole races of barbarians were taken into the church in bulk, and bore the name of Christ while they practiced their old life and hugged their ancestral customs. They, of necessity, lowered the standard of the church, and it soon became the accepted teaching that membership in the church insured salvation, which meant an escape from hell and an ultimate entrance into heaven. Everybody knows now how this conception fostered immorality and made the church a whited sepulchre, full of corruption.

Some of the revival work of our own day has erred in the same direction. It has consciously or unconsciously given the impression that a man can become *saved* without becoming *changed*. Any encouragement in that direction is recruit work for the enemy of souls. A burning ship is not saved simply by having a tugboat fasten to it and tow it along over the swelling sea. It is saved by having the fire put out, so that it can pursue its course, whether long or short, to its desired haven. A man in whom the old fire is burning, who hugs his idols, and loves the same things he has always loved, cannot be saved by joining a church, or by groaning, or by saying he hopes he has found mercy. There is no limit to the mercy, and anybody can find it who really seeks it, but the mercy cannot reach him effectively until he is ready to cut all the cables of his old life, and take God as his choice above everything else. The saved man is a changed man; the change begins within, and works out through him and penetrates every fibre of his being. We are not primarily after numbers or after more church members. We are carrying Christ to those who are "out of Him," and we must not rest satisfied with any soul until it finds Him and He possesses it.

CHAPTER XLVIII

CHRISTIAN HOLINESS

THERE are many Christians who do not believe in the doctrine of holiness, and who can hardly conceive of such a state in this life, though they expect to be perfectly holy as soon as they enter heaven. They look with pity or perhaps with disgust upon those who declare that holiness is intended as a state of life right here in the midst of sin and temptation, and they consider *that* as making life altogether too serious.

Holiness has never been a popular doctrine, for it implies the destruction of all the old idols which fill a very large place in the life and thought of mankind, and it generally seems, though most people would not confess it in plain words, that life would be pretty empty WITH ONLY GOD.

But we cannot find any other teaching in the New Testament than this, that God expects men to be holy here in this world. There is no hint that any other kind of life is possible for the Christian. With Christ the choice is always between the undivided life with Him or a rejection of Him. He knows nothing of that method, which very many try to make successful, of carrying the world in one hand and holding Christ with the other. It is a perversion of the text, "Let not thy left hand know what the right hand doeth."

But the real reason that very many people fail to be influenced by the teaching of holiness is that they know nothing of it except as a *doctrine*. They do not behold it manifested in a life, and they demand *facts* before they will be convinced. We must accept this test. No one can expect that his teaching of holiness will make much impression if at the same time he does not illustrate the doctrine in his life.

In all teaching, experiment makes more impression than lecturing does, for truth is caught by the eye more easily than by the ear.

People are not hungry for theology in our day, and they pay very little attention to cold and logical doctrine. They, however, are ready to be convinced by positive facts, and there never was a time in the world when more people would believe in experimental holiness than now.

The person who under all circumstances and all testing gives the true ring and shows no flaw, who is satisfied with *just* God and has no ulterior purpose, who amid all the currents of life points straight toward the pole, such a person quietly knocks the props from under skepticism, for no one can doubt what he really sees.

It is wonderfully easy to hold a doctrine after you have once made up your mind to it, but to prove your faith by living out the doctrine in your life is the hard thing. Most people prefer to postpone holiness for heaven, where it will be easy. But it is a fatal mistake to make. It is just as unwise as for a student to postpone his study until examination time. This life is admirably fitted to train the spiritual athlete and test him at every point. A cloud of witnesses surround us as we bend forward toward the goal, but there is no victory for him who will not lay aside all weights and cast from him the sins which are like close-fitting garments to beset him.

Holiness is not a theory any more than health is,—it is a condition of life. A person is holy only when he fulfills the conditions and enters into the life, and then there will be no chance for deception, for the fruits of holiness are as distinct and real as the fruit of vine or tree.

If we want to be powerful teachers of the doctrine of holiness we must simply be holy;

there is no other way to teach it. And we must be careful not to deceive anybody into thinking he is holy when he is not, for it is infinitely worse than making a man think he is well when he is sick.

CHAPTER XLIX

THE FOUNDING OF THE CHURCH

THE Gospels do not set forth simply God's purpose for the individual life; in fact it is one of the deepest truths of life that no man can live unto himself.

The first confession of personal faith—made by Peter near Cæsarea Philippi, to the fact that Jesus is the Christ, the Son of God—was the occasion for the announcement of a purpose reaching beyond the individual—namely, the building of a church—a permanent Christian structure in the world.

This famous passage in Matt. 16: 18-19, is the text which has formed the basis for the papal system, and it is inscribed in gigantic letters on the dome of St. Peter's Cathedral, in Rome, as the absolute authority for an infallible earthly vice-gerent of Christ. Strangely enough, this text which unfolds the Saviour's conception of a Christian fellowship of individual responsibility and freedom has been made a proof text for the worst religious tyranny in history. It is really a magna charta of spiritual liberty, it has been made a warrant for the establishment of an unlimited despotism, which leaves no soul free access to God.

Let us consider the meaning of the passage which more than any other reveals Christ's thought concerning the church fellowship which He purposed to found, to continue the work which He personally began.

He was on His way to Jerusalem for the last time. His words in Galilee had convinced the people that He had not come to fulfil *their* Messianic hope. He had told them that His kingdom was a spiritual one, and not a glorified revival of the Israelitish monarchy. His followers began to drop off, and it became only too evident that the people were not ready for His messages of eternal life

The disciples tell Him in answer to His question that the general impression is that He is a prophet—Elias, Jeremiah—but no one ranks Him higher than these great figures of Jewish history. "But whom say ye that I am?" "Thou are the Christ, the son of the living God," answers Peter. It is the first spontaneous confession of faith that He is the Divine One and, as Jesus said, it was no superficial statement, but a conviction revealed in the heart by the Spirit, a revelation from the

Father and not a conjecture of the brain—"Flesh and blood hath not revealed this to thee."

Then follows the answer: "Thou art Peter and on this rock I will build my church, and the gates of Hades shall not prevail against it. I will give unto thee the keys of the kingdom of heaven. Whatsoever thou shall bind on earth shall be bound in heaven, and whatsoever thou shalt loose on earth shall be loosed in heaven." It means that as this man's personal faith in Christ as the son of God has wrought in him a transformation of heart and life, and made good that early promise that he should one day be Peter—a rock—so on this very rock-nature which is Christ-formed, the visible church is to be builded. In the midst of a disbelieving world there is at least one man who can be a nucleus for the Christian fellowship; for coming unto the living stone, He Himself has been made a lively stone, and of such the church is to be built. This first living believer is to become a center of spiritual power to call into existence a whole community of believers in Christ; not as the offical bishop of Rome, but as the recipient of Pentecostal fire and spiritual power.

The church is, then, to be a community of brothers who have individually, by a similar faith and confession, seen Christ as the Son of God—in whom, as in Peter, the vital transformation shows the rock character forming—men and women who are living stones through union with the Rock of Ages.

The sole qualification for authority is the evidence of special spiritual power, and that is what the bestowal of the keys means. It is decidedly not an authority of official position, but an authority which rests wholly upon personal faith and deep spiritual character. To Peter, and to every man who has by a like faith gained a similar spiritual insight, Christ confers power in the kingdom—authority in the direction of the propagation of the truths of the Gospel.

Whatever such a community of spiritually-enlightened believers, gathered in the name of Christ, and agreeing together in an agreement born of the mind and spirit of Christ shall ask, it shall be given; for under such conditions they could ask for nothing which was not heaven-prompted; and furthermore, whatsoever under those conditions they shall "bind or loose," shall be bound and loosed in heaven.

"Binding and loosing" are expressions which the rabbis of the time constantly used in the sense of declaring something *forbidden* or *permitted*. The idea conveyed in the famous passage is that those who compose the community of believers, the citizens of the kingdom, acting in the name of Christ and in His power, are authorized to determine what is consistent and what is inconsistent with fellowship in the church—what is to be permitted and what is to be forbidden. It gives no occasion for lordship and tyranny, but it makes the clarified, illumined souls who have unhindered access to God through Christ by the one Spirit, the bearers of the keys—the centers of authority.

Acting on this authority, the apostolic church "loosed" circumcision, but "bound" fidelity to the marriage vow. They "loosed" the Jewish Sabbath, but "bound" the fitting observance of the Lord's day. They "loosed" Mosaic sacrifices, but "bound" the necessity of a living faith in Him who is a High Priest forever after the order of Melchisedec.

This conception of the church—and it certainly is Christ's conception of it—would make it impossible for the church ever to be fossilized or its truth crytalized. Christ conceives the church as a vital organism, and as such it must be progressive—i. e., it must successively adapt itself to the changed conditions of society, and make its message drawing and vitalizing as new situations confront it. Its message of redemption from sin and of new life in Christ, is an eternal message, for the need of this is, and will remain, a continuous need; but for all practical matters and for all its methods and practices, the body itself, under the immediate guidance of the Head of the church, is commissioned with authority —an authority, however, which comes not through an unbroken line of historic bishops, but which comes from the fact that the individuals composing the structure are living stones set upon the living Foundation. This idea of organic union with Christ is again and again taught in the New Testament, and it is put as a necessary condition for bearing fruit. Christians cannot perform their functions if they try to live an exclusive life. Union with Christ brings all Christians into a oneness of organism like that of the branches of a vine. The promise that Christ's followers should do even greater works than He did, is followed by the significant words: "In that day shall ye know that I am in my Father and ye in me and I in you." That is a union and incorporation which would make a powerful church. Why do not we have it at once? Because the bulk of Christians have, strangely enough, made little of this idea of corporate union with Christ and with one another, and have instead divided their forces by petty differences of opinion on things that have no vital effect upon the condition of the soul, such as whether one can preach authoritatively without a surplice, whether water should be put on the man or the man put in the water, whether the external communion should be a common meal or an individual partaking of bread and wine. No wonder that Paul, who knew—if any man ever did—the meaning of this vital union with Christ, cried out: "The kingdom of God is not meat and drink, but righteousness and peace and joy in the Holy Ghost;" and again, "Neither circumcision nor uncircumcision availeth anything but a new creation." This is a key-note of New Testament Christianity—a new creation, a new creation for each soul, and a new creation for society. In other words, it is the fulfilment of the Divine purpose, "Let us make man in our own image."

CHAPTER L

THE GOSPEL OF THE KINGDOM

CHRISTIANITY is not a new philosophy. It is a "way of life," and this expression was the common name for the new religion among its early adherents—"Those of the Way." Again it is called, "The power of God unto salvation;" that is, it is a revelation of God's power at work in the world to save men and to fit them for higher ends. It is the evangel of the kingdom, as it always appears in the parables of Christ. It is, in the simplest statement, God's plan to reconstruct man and society, and it is this sense, it seems to us, that Christ uses the great expression, "Kingdom of Heaven," "Kingdom of God," "the Kingdom," "My Kingdom." It is the perfect, original order of things which has its home in heaven, coming down from hence and realizing itself on the earth; it is the ideal condition of humanity, existing first only in God's thought, and then wrought out by Him as an existing fact; it is the realized sway of God as the beginning and end of all things.

The expression was a common one to the Jews of the period, and John the Baptist's cry, "the kingdom of heaven is at hand," meant to those who heard it the setting up of the temporal messianic kingdom under a king who should break all foreign yokes and make Israel in very truth the people of God. They conceived a kingdom which should perfect the law and ceremonies, which should make the Temple, the holy of holies, the central spot of the globe. Their fundamental idea was the establishment of an Israelitish theocracy, which should extend itself politically over all the nations, as Rome had extended its sway. Christ, however, never ceased to declare and demonstrate that he had not come to break the Roman yoke or establish a Jewish supremacy. Little by little it dawned upon the disciples that this kingdom of which they so often heard from their Master's lips was totally unlike the "perishable husk" for which the people yearned. It was not a thing of "lo here or lo there;" it was not the establishment of a new external kingship, or the setting up of a more perfect Temple service and a purified ritual, but the proclamation of a new life to be entered by a birth from above— a fact which the great Jewish lawyer, Nicodemus, could not possibly comprehend. It

comes whenever a soul yields to the wooing of
God, and lets His light break in. It establishes itself not in a temple or a capital city,
but in a heart that yields to the sway of the
King. The kingdom itself is perfect as it
exists in the thought of God, and if it could
have been realized by a magic act and set up
ready made, Christ's work could have been
finished in a moment, but it was rather God's
plan to realize the kingdom on the earth progressively—to draw men to it by Grace and
Love, and to increase its realm by silent victories over soul after soul, and then to make
each transformed soul a propagator of the new
life and power to other souls. Its conquests
are never by force or compulsion, but by the
diffusion of light, by the manifestation of love,
by awakening hunger for righteousness. You
may know that it is at work in the world
when you see evil defeated and corruption
cleansed away. "Where the carcass is there
are the vultures," said Christ,—*i. e.*, wherever
the old dead and corrupt things appear there
are scavengers to remove it and make the air
wholesome and pure. As God provides ways
of keeping His world clean, so you may see
the kingdom coming when evil is put down
in a life and Christian graces appear; whenever a corrupt custom is purged away, when-

ever a sinner is changed into a saint, whenever sin is conquered by the power of God the circle of the kingdom widens, and the truth of Christ's many parables of illustration is proved to all who have eyes to see and ears to hear.

The setting up of this kingdom is not the work of a day or of a year, but the kingdom is like a man who sowed seed in his field and slept, and rose night and day and the seed grew, he knew not how, first the blade, then the ear, then the full corn in the ear.

But the fundamental conception of the kingdom of God, as made known in our Gospels, is the truth that it is founded on purity of heart—a heart-purity which is attained only through apprehension of Christ, the Son of God, as the revealer of sin, the redeemer from sin, and through the indwelling and life of God by the Holy Spirit. It is a kingdom in which blessedness comes only with holiness. Every beatitude attaches to a condition of the heart, and can be realized in no other way. No performance of any acts or ceremonials which custom and tradition have authorized and rendered sacred, can in the slightest degree affect one's standing before God. The pure in heart, the meek, the poor in spirit, the peacemaker, the thirster after righteousness—all these have a condition of heart to which a blessing of God immediately follows, as the rain falls when the air is saturated to the deposit point. But the fasting and praying and giving of alms of the Pharisee on the other hand, as well as his scrupulous washings and purifications, his avoidance of all things ceremonially unclean, his spirit of self-righteousness, and his hard, mean nature are far beneath the standard of admission to the kingdom of heaven. "Unless your righteousness exceed the righteousness of the scribes and pharisees ye shall in no wise enter." This means that the Gospel knows nothing of an acquired goodness—a goodness of effort a goodness which is put on from the outside—which fits for the kingdom. It is a changed heart, a cleansed life, a transformed nature, a purified being which is required.

CHAPTER LI

THE TEST OF CHRISTIANITY

WE have learned that it is never safe to estimate the worth and value of a man by the number of cubits which measure his stature. No foot-rule test gives the real capacity of a man, because personality cannot be measured by the yard.

Nevertheless the similar mistake is continually made of estimating a man's Christianity by some such inadequate foot-rule test. It would be well for us, if we could, to get back to the standards of Christ and the Apostles and see how they tested religion. The question never is, What kind of a coat do you wear? or what are your "views" on creation and sin and inspiration? or what do you think about the Sacraments? In fact, Christ never asked a man a theological question during his whole ministry. "Art thou desiring to be made whole?" "Dost thou love God with all thy heart and thy neighbor as thyself? "Go and sin no more." "Her sins are forgiven, for she loved much," are some of the wonderful words which came from His lips when He was dealing with individual cases. When the Jews tried to catch Him with metaphysical and theological questions, such as "what sin caused this man to be blind?" or "whose wife will this woman be in the resurrection?" He immediately brushed away the fruitless abstractions and gave clear, practical answers: "This blind man is an occasion for the exhibition of God's power"—*i.e.*, for working a work of God, and "If you read the Scriptures aright you would understand that God is the God of the living, and that you must not measure the heavenly life by the limitations of the earthly life."

John's tests of Christianity are quite different from those which we use to-day. He again makes no reference to things which we consider tests of soundness: "Every one that loveth is born of God." "We know that we have passed from death to life because we love." "We know that we dwell in Him, because we have His Spirit." "Whatsoever is born of God overcometh the world." "Whosoever is born of God sinneth not." "He that hath the Son of God hath life."

It can be quickly seen that these are no light and easy tests, and that a man who could answer all our articles of belief and make a great display of theological orthodoxy, might at the same time fail in every point of John's tests. He that loveth, he that has the Spirit in his heart and life, he that overcometh the world, he that does not commit sin—what a sifting!

Now there has been and still is great danger of making so much of theological tests of soundness that these deeper, truer and more spiritual tests—which are the only ones of importance to Christ and the Apostles—should be overlooked. There are Christians to-day who decide upon a man's Christianity by his intellectual opinions and conclusions, rather than by the spiritual condition of his heart and his life, though it is an unscriptural position to take. The end and aim of religion—we cannot say it too often—is to bring men to God and to make them Christlike, and religion has never done its perfect work in a man until it fills his life with the Holy Spirit and his heart with love. Right belief upon questions which directly affect the spiritual life is tremendously important, and faith is the very hand by which we grasp and appropriate the divine realities; but we have no more right to rule men out of Christ's kingdom on the test of an intellectual shibboleth than we have to count devils in, simply because they believe and tremble. The time has come when men's minds must be left free to look at every fact in God's world, and to come to the best conclusions they can upon them, and we must estimate their Christianity by New Testament tests, which are invariably spiritual tests, and measure the life and faith by Christ's standards.

CHAPTER LII

THE MESSAGE OF QUAKERISM

EVERY great religious movement starts out of some single fundament religious principle, but if it is to have extensive and permanent effect upon human society, it must ultimately ramify and illumine the whole realm of thought and the entire range of life and activity. The significant periods of history are those ages when men have caught a new and clearer glimpse of God and have set their lives by new and higher standards. There is a widely accepted theory that the true religion is forever fixed and unchangeable. It is a rigid system of doctrines, mysteriously communicated, not to be questioned by reason, to be accepted by faith and to be guarded as the absolute truth, crystalized into a form suited to every age and every race of men.

A very slight study of history undermines that theory. The moment a religion becomes only a system of thought or a crystalized truth, its service to the world is over, it can no longer feed living souls, for it offers only a stone where bread is asked; and furthermore, such a religion becomes a dangerous hindrance to the advance of truth and a menace to a free access of the individual soul to its living God. On the contrary, religion can never become a fixed and unchangeable thing, for religion is the soul's life in God and its response to Him; and therefore it must be as free as life, and it will have its high tides and its low, its ebbs and its floods, as history shows us has been the fact.

Religion always begins with a manifestation, a revelation of God and the soul's answer to it. Heathen religions sprung from a sense of awe awakened in the presence of manifestations of power, in thunder and lightning, in mighty storms, in sun-rise, in the rush of a great river, in the sublimity of the dome of the sky. The Christian religion begins with the revelation of God's *love*, in an Incarnation, in a Personality.

> "Think, Abib, dost thou think?
> So, the All-Great were the All-Loving too—
> So, through the thunder comes a human voice
> Saying, ' O heart I made, a heart beats here!
> Face, my hands have fashioned, see it in myself!
> Thou hast no power, nor may'st conceive of mine,
> But love I gave thee, with myself to love
> And thou must love me who have died for thee!'" *

---

* "An Epistle."—Robert Browning.

Christianity begins with the appearance of a Being who is genuinely human so that he can speak to human conditions and genuinely Divine so that he can reveal God. This revelation through Personality—the Word made flesh—shows the Divine thought *i. e.* that man was meant to be in the Divine image, to be a son, and it shows the Divine heart beating for us in our errors, our struggles, our sins. The whole gospel is summed up in the story of the Prodigal who comes to himself and goes to the Father and finds His love still warm and His arms still out for the embrace that welcomes to sonship. Christianity, then, was meant to be a free river to grace and life flowing from God through human lives and making all things new.

It soon crystalized into a church that was partially paganized by contact with the old world. It shut out all approach to God except through its narrow channels. It claimed that God could speak only through the hierarchy of priests, that grace could come only through certain fixed sacraments, that truth could be found only in one book. God became a distant being, Christ became a mystical messenger from Him to found an infallible Church. The Virgin and the saints became the real intercessors between human hearts and the distant God. The glowing truths given to the world at such tremendous cost and sacrifice hardened into cold dogmas which had to be accepted on pain of condemnation for heresy and those who thought were forced to agree with the interpretations of the past or to stop thinking altogether. The world sank into decrepitude, a condition still preserved in Spain. Christianity seemed dying a natural death. Then came an age of awakening, an emancipation. A new world was discovered. Printing was invented and books were made for rich and poor alike. Copernicus made a complete revolution of thought by his discovery that the sun is the centre of our system of worlds, and the earth only a planet which revolves about it. This discovery made modern science possible. Luther inaugurated another revolution in thought in his profound spiritual discovery that "justification is by faith." It seemed a simple truth, but it broke the power and dominion of the Latin Church and exalted at once the importance of the individual. Each man stands in an individual relation to God and he is responsible directly for his soul and for his faith. Protestantism is the gospel of individuality. Like the discovery of Copernicus, it finds a new centre. Before, everything revolved about the Church and the hierarchy. Henceforth, Christ is the centre and each man's orbit is determined by his relation to Christ. But it was impossible for the Reformers to break entirely with the historic Church. They were the creatures of their age, and their roots had grown deep in the soil of mediæval thought. The time had not then come, perhaps it has not yet fully come for the realization of the Christian ideal. But in the middle of the 17th century in England, an honest effort was made to set forth a constructive principle which should transform man and society and which, when worked out in practical life should affect the entire race, and it contains, I believe, the seeds of apostolic Christianity transplanted in new soil and after long centuries of waiting.

The central note of Quakerism, as it was originally promulgated, is the truth that man's salvation and higher life are personal matters between the individual soul and God, that the living Christ brings the soul into newness of life in Him, and that there is a clear witness of the fact established in the consciousness of the believer and in his changed life and nature. It is what the Apostle calls "the demonstration of the spirit."

It is the kind of evidence a man has of light when he opens his eyes and the sunlight streams in. It is the kind of evidence an artist has of beauty when he stands caught by the glory of a sunset; it is the kind of evidence an experimenter has of the power of electricity when the current from the dynamo thrills through him to the ends of his fingers and the roots of his hair. It is an evidence not from external authority but from the immediate perception of the soul. Paul dates his religious life from an experience which he compares to a *fiat lux* of creation. "God," he says, "shined into our hearts to give the light of the knowledge of the glory of God in the face of Jesus Christ." In language which means almost precisely the same thing, George Fox dates his religious crisis. "When all my hope was gone so that I had nothing outward to help me, then O! then, I heard a voice which said 'There is one, even Jesus Christ, that can speak to thy condition' and when I heard it my heart did leap for joy." The whole spiritual life springs immediately from God and that is why there is no danger that religion will come to an end. So long as God continues to surround our lives and break in upon sensitive hearts, there will be those who find in Christ an incarnation of God who is near us all and who only waits for a window to open when his light breaks in and makes life seem clear and real. As Sabatier has said, men are "incurably religious," and sincere and earnest souls will continue to find God and know Him when He reveals Himself to to them in the face of Jesus Christ. We live in an age when the worth and meaning of everything are tested. We do not care how old a theory is, or how sacred it was in the middle ages; we ask at once, is it true? Does it meet our need, does it speak to our condition? Now the message of Quakerism carries men beyond the props and scaffoldings and stands them face to face with a living God. It declares that men were meant for God and that a man can never be his true self until God possesses him. That his darkness is made, like that of the earth, because he lives in his own shadow. Wheel about and the light fronts you, and has been shining all the time. You made your own darkness. Now, no amount of ceremony or of subscription to theological dogmas will save a man who still keeps his face away from God, and still lives in the dark while he is holding in his lean hands the rags of his external profession. Life, religion, sonship begin with the creation of a new man within a man, and there is no substitute for this. The Christian religion is not a theory, not a plan, not a scheme, but a dynamic force, *i.e.* the power of God unto salvation, and every soul who comes to himself and goes to the Father has a more immediate consciousness of God as a reality than the most philosophical man has of the reality of the earth on which his feet stand, for the earth must always be a foreign object of inference, while the Quaker message tells of a Christ who becomes a part of our very life and "is closer to us than breathing, nearer than hands and feet." There, then, the Quaker message comes with sure help to our agnostic age, to men who have seen the old land marks vanish one by one. It begins by saying, put Christianity to a practical test. Try it as you try the great laws of science. How do you know that the law of gravitation is true? You feel it tug upon you. You see every particle of matter in the visible universe obey it. It swings satellites and planets before your eyes. It draws the whole ocean and dashes it up the beach twice each day. You cannot doubt it. How do you know there is any spiritual power, any Divine truth, any God of love, any Christ who can redeem from sin? There is only one sure test. Try it. Throw yourself on God as you plant your foot on the rock. Act as though God walked by your side every minute. Turn your face to Christ, follow Him, obey every gleam of light you get. Set yourself stubbornly against every shadow of a sin that crosses your track and resolve that if there is a God in the universe, you will find Him, know Him, love Him. The result is—the testimony is universal—the soul that does that always finds God, always does get led into the truth, always does become renewed and transformed. Quakerism builds upon this demonstration of the Spirit, and in so doing, it is in harmony with all the great leaders of modern philosophy, notably, DesCartes, Kant, Fichte and Hegel, all of whom build their systems on the immediate testimony of self-consciousness. No discovery of science, no conclusion of criticism, no possible advances of thought, no separations by time from Divine transactions on which the historic Church is builded, can for a moment endanger this immediate and dynamic faith. In place of external sacraments, which at best could never be more than outward symbols of some reality, and which could only have had a use in the transition period when the Church was hampered by its Jewish swaddling clothes, the Quaker message substitutes an efficient baptism, a direct incoming of Divine forces for the transformation and control of the whole man, and a feeding of the soul with spiritual bread which shows its effect in deepened life and an ever increased spirituality.

This means, then, that the Quaker message is a call for a perfected man and a perfected society. It builds on the belief that man was not meant to live in sin. That salvation does not mean a scheme for escaping the penalty due for our sins; but it is a power by which we are enabled to destroy sin itself, subdue it, put it down, triumph over it in the strength of a new life which comes from participation in the Life—the Vine of which we should be organic branches. Its goal is to put man in the condition Adam was in before he fell, or rather into a higher condition still, for the man who has faced the moral struggle, who has tasted the tree of knowledge of good and evil, and has through Divine grace won his way upward to the shining height where he is a king and priest—crowned and mitered—is almost inconceivably higher than a being that has not yet felt the tug of temptation.

Quakerism does not limit the promulgation of this truth to any single channel. It draws no hard and fast line between clergy and laity. Every person, whether male or female, who receives the demonstration of the Spirit and finds himself joined the Lord, as a member, is a propagator of this holy order, this spiritual society, this City of God, this Kingdom of Heaven, this priesthood of saints.

It is not dependent for its faith on anything which investigation or criticism can touch or weaken. We stake our whole case on the fact that our lives are circled by the Divine Life, that the Christ who was in the flesh at a definite period of history is a living Christ and forms Himself within all souls who turn to Him, that religion begins with an immediate consciousness of our need of Him and a voluntary choosing that He shall be our Redeemer and Controler. It mounts higher and higher as our creative faith lays hold of Him as a present reality and works its effects in transformation, in victory over sin, in manifest power, in fruits of character and the production of Christlikeness. Out of this consciousness of Christ, already found and His will revealed to us, we have an absolute ground to build on.

Every line of Revelation, every lesson of history, helps us see God's purpose. In the New Testament we have revealed the life and mission of the Christ who still works as of old. We see there the Divine Heart, His sorrow for sin, His method of redemption, His idea of society, His estimate of the worth of man. This whole story unfolds with overwhelming power upon those who know its truth in the experience of their own lives, for it comes as the word of the Father whom the child knows already. Everything about this religion is vital. Its test is life; it begins in a birth; it proves itself true by its increasing life and it is as sure of eternity as God is, for it is what it is through living union in Him.

This is a religion which not only makes us sure of heaven ultimately, but free in the truth *now*, conscious of His forgiveness and immediate presence *now*, able to withstand temptation *now*, victorious over sin *now*, possessed of peace and secure from fears *now*, triumphant in the power of the living spirit and in present possession of an earnest of eternal life.

We are not called to the *other* wordly but *this* wordly. Here is our sphere, here is our arena. We are not to stand gazing up into heaven. We are rather to build in our layer in the walls of a new Jerusalem here on the earth. Our knighthood is not to be spent, or our spurs won in searching for some mystical Holy Grail, some sacred cup which would heal disease, and transform society and usher in the new and perfect order, if we could only find it. We are rather called to manifest the power of God in a practical Christian life. Let disease and misery find from our own hands a healing and comforting touch. Let the sore-tempted and erring learn from our life how sin can be conquered and victory gained. May our faith burn and glow so that some hard beset and doubting one may kindle his faith from ours. Let our fight with sin and evil and corruption be so genuine and strenuous that we shall use only the weapons of righteousness and truth. Let us never forget that we are serving God and truly engaged in religious service when we are working and struggling to uplift and enlighten mankind, and to create a better and a truer citizenship and a cleaner political life.

Religion is not a one-seated chariot, with horses of fire to carry us safely to heaven above and apart from the din and the stress of this imperfect world. The palm and the robe are won by the saints who fight the good fight and lift at the real burdens of the world.

It is a part of our business to demonstrate that modern thought, and scholarly research do not undermine religion and that Christianity is not outdated and superseded. We must stand for and illustrate a type of Christianity which affects and vitalizes the whole man, which animates and vivifies every strata of society and which expands to meet the growing need of the world.

Instead of closing our eyes let us see all the facts and go where the truth leads us. So long as God reigns and our Alpha and Omega is alive forever more we are not going to suffer shipwreck simply because we are discovering that some of the notions which the mediæval church taught us must be revised in the light of further thought. It used to be believed that the earth rested on an elephant and the elephant on the back of a tortoise. Alas, we have had to give up this childish theory, and now we find that nothing holds us, except an invisible and intangible power of gravitation, whatever that may be! But who would prefer an elephant and tortoise and who feels afraid that this unseen cord will break or that something will unbind the sweet influence of the pleiades or loose the bands of orion?

Little by little we have been pushed back from one material outpost to another until at last we find that our faith must ultimately rest upon an invisible and intangible God, an impalpable Spirit of Life and Love, who never writes on the sky with His finger, who never shows His face to telescope or microscope, who never lets us catch Him at work.

> " Whose dwelling is the light of setting suns,
> And the round ocean, and the living air,
> And the blue sky and in the mind of man—

> A motion and a spirit that impels
> All thinking things, all objects of all thought,
> And rolls through all things."

But who that has seen the light of the knowledge of the glory of God in the face of Jesus Christ, who that has felt his own heart drawn by that manifestation of Love, who that has had his own life transformed and made victorious by that spiritual power wants the material sign, or feels afraid for his religion because he has only God left? No, the foundation stands sure, having this seal, the Lord knoweth them that are his. Let us

> "Correct the portrait by the living face,
> Man's God by God's God in the mind of man."

CHAPTER LIII.

THE EFFECT OF DISCOURAGEMENT

FEW of us realize how much our view of things is affected by our sense of success or of defeat. People who are continually prosperous, and who have no knowledge of the dead strain of pushing on in the face of insuperable obstacles, naturally have different views of life from those who tug day after day at a great burden which their human hands cannot roll off, and who see failure and defeat follow their best efforts. The successful man finds it hard to sympathize with those who are steadily unsuccessful, for he cannot put himself in their place, he cannot possibly feel as they feel, and consequently he does not understand how they can hold such views.

Consciously or unconsciously, our ideas of God and of heaven, and all our religious conceptions, grow colored as we look out through successes or through defeats. The theology of the Puritan was in harmony with the gloom and struggle which filled such a place in his life. He found himself in a world where the good seemed to be defeated by the bad, in a world where everything had to be gained by desperate struggle with manifold enemies, and the sunshine of life went out, the gloom settled down, and out of his view of life came his idea of God and of the unseen world.

We are told over and over again that we must not let the things of life affect us, that we must throw off our burdens and quit ourselves like men even though difficulties crowd thick about us. And this is right. The true Christian may pray earnestly to have his thorn in the flesh removed, but whether it is removed or not, he will learn that there is sufficient grace to enable him to get a rich blessing even out of the ever present thorn, yet in spite of himself he will not see things in the same light as though no thorn had come to him. A person with a whole body, free from pain or ache, and with tireless vigor for all the calls and duties of life, cannot see things just as one does who is hindered in every effort by a body which constantly makes its weakness felt, and which quivers with pains that cannot be removed. Humanly speaking, the defeat that brings discouragement, and the bodily disabilities which fasten upon us, make life take on a color which otherwise it would not have; but as there could be no rainbow of promise without a cloud or without the falling rain so, often, the richest colors of our life are made out of the very things which at first seem to shut down over us and completely darken us. A person's real success depends on how he can make use of his trials.

There is no rainbow without sunshine and no man can see a bow of hope and promise in the dark things of life unless he has somewhere a source of light. There is something magnificent in the way the early Christians painted the clouds with pictures of hope and images of glory, but it was because of the brightness of the light which came from their Christ. The only way any one can keep his life and thought from being warped and distorted by defeats and hindrances is to have the "mind of Christ" which kept Paul's faith so clear and vital amid difficulties which would have crushed a self centered man. In Christ there is no defeat. In Christ a man may rise victorious over the thorn which enters deepest into the flesh.

This may sound like preaching, and may seem to some a good theory, but an impossibility for experience. We write it as one of the clearest facts of Christian experience, and one of the essential truths of the Gospel of Christ.

The Christianity which does not make a person victorious has an essential element left out. It is no especial glory that a man's Christianity keeps him strong when he is on the floodtide of prosperity; it is its glory that it can send light and strength into the darkest hour of seeming defeat.

CHAPTER LIV

LEARNING TO LIVE IN A NEW WORLD

OFTEN we sit and wonder, after a dear one has left us through the gate of death, how it would seem to go through and wake up on the other side! It is hard to imagine the life and scenery in a world entirely new. We always catch ourselves carrying our old experiences into everything which we try to picture. Before we visit a new place we vaguely construct an image of it in the mind, built out of descriptions which we have heard, and filled in with our own memories of similar places. But when we actually arrive, we are apt to say, "This is entirely different from anything I imagined." If that is the case with earthly scenes, how certainly must it be so with that country from which no traveler has returned with reports, and of which "no sociable angel has breathed an early syllable."

What are the experiences of the newly-parted soul? Is it true, as a great poet sings, that the soul, once through the "blessed gate," sees

> "In a fountain fresh,
> All knowledge that the sons of flesh
> Shall gather in the cycled times."

Does that vast world of the spirit, with its heights and depths, its lengths and its breadths, break upon the newcomer, from the land of rocks and hills and trees, all at once? Does he feel at home, and join immediately in the activities of the long-accustomed citizens of that city? Or does he, rather, slowly learn the riches of the new realm, and the manners of its inhabitants? Who can give the answer? No one feels himself a bold expert in this field. But is there not something to be learned from the newly-arrived in *this* world?

The room into which the baby is born is crammed with love. The hearts of father and mother are swelling with emotion. Love is there before he arrives; affection is ripe before he appears. He comes to an intimate circle all waiting for him, and his first cry stirs one of the deepest joys which this earth of ours ever gives a mortal to feel. He has indeed come to his own. Does the little new-born appreciate it all and tell how glad he is to be on these shores among such kindly people, and amid such happy scenes? Not at all. Love is something new and strange. He had not learned it in the other world where he was. It takes some time to discover how wonderful it is and to be able to contribute his part of love to the happy circle around him. He learns it because it is the very atmosphere into which he has come. Those who were there ahead of him teach it to him as fast as he is able to learn, until, like his own small circle, he, too, is ripe in love.

Think, too, how little the newcomer knows of the size of the world he has come into. His tiny body has formed itself in most narrow and contracted quarters. There was not a bit of wasted space. He has come from a world meant only for one, and he touched all the sides of his nutshell of a realm. Here he is now in a universe which has no limits. The room seems at first a whole world. But it is not. It is only one room in a larger house, and the house is only one house in a larger city, and the city is in a State, and the State is in a nation, and the nation is in a continent, and the continent is in a world, and the world is in a solar system, and the solar system is in an immeasurably spacious universe.

How impossible for those little blinking eyes, too weak for one glance at the sun, to take in all this. He must slowly spell out the wonders of his new home. Those who have learned ahead of him will teach him as fast as the mind can comprehend. There is no contrast greater than that between the first home of the unborn and the second home into which birth brings the minute life. But does any one suppose that the soul, freed from the limits and constraints of body altogether, will have less sweeping changes of life and scenery? Contrasts increase as we mount. The higher the life the higher correspondingly is the environment of it. Here we have infinities of space, there we shall find new kinds of infinity, now unimaginable. Here we learn the meaning of the "group-love" into which we are born, there we shall learn the inconceivably higher spiritual qualities of the realm, so near, yet so unknown. One thing is sure, where much has to be guessed, when we *wake* there, and learn what we have come to, we shall be *satisfied!*

CHAPTER LV

BEHIND THE GATE

I WAS walking along a traveled highway one summer day, and in the distance I saw a little four-year-old child standing by a great iron gate which closed up the entrance to the child's home. The little thing wanted to get in and couldn't. She pounded in vain with her little fist against the hopelessly impassable iron barrier. She rattled the great latch, but that did no good. Again she pounded and pushed, but the iron gate stood unmoved and hardly felt a shiver or a jar. Suddenly she realized that the task was hopeless, that she had no powers at all to get beyond the impenetrable gate. It would not let her through. She burst into an agony of weeping and cried as though her little heart would break. The wail of sorrow did its work. Hastily the gate was pulled open, the little child was caught up by the mother's loving arms and the tears were kissed away. "Didn't you know I would come and let you in as soon as I could? Now it's all right. Don't cry a bit more."

Does any one want a better parable of life than that? How many of us stand before barriers as unyielding as the great iron gate and beat with all our might as the little child who wanted to get through? We cannot see around or under or over. No voice answers back when we call. Our push and stroke of hand are as vain and feeble to move the gate which stretches between us and those we seek as the little four-year-old's tiny fist against the hard iron. But the love behind *our* gate is every bit as real as that which the little child found when her cry reached through.

Does any one suppose that mothers care when their little ones have pain, that they run to lift the hard latch and bring in their beaten and baffled children, and yet that God doesn't care when His children stand with bruised and wounded hands before the great doors which they cannot open? Nay, not so. Every word of revelation which has come from God says "No." *Like as a father pitieth his children so the Lord doeth toward His own. A mother may forget her nursing babe, but I do not forget. Not a sparrow falleth without the Father's notice; of how much more value are ye? Let not your heart be troubled. I am behind the gate preparing a place for you; if it were not so I would have told you.*

But does some perplexed soul cry out, "Why should there be any gate? why may we not see through and discover the stretched-out arms and realize that all is to come out as we wish?" Because all our highest blessings and our supremely precious gains come through faith and not through sight. The whole training and discipline of life demand some mysteries and some strain and stretch of heart. If every gate swung open at our touch, and no hard crying and deep yearning were ever necessary, we should be infinitely poorer creatures and not fit for God's heaven when it opened to us. Those who wear the white and carry the palms have *come up* through hard testing, and have trod the wine press of suffering with Him whose blood made them white.

CHAPTER LVI

SOME STRANGE TRIUMPHAL CHARIOTS

MANY of us have come through the year just closing with the marks of the struggle upon us. When it opened on New Year's morning we were happy in our powers and in our possesions, and thought perhaps only of the rosy outlook of another year of joy. Now it is closing, and we look back upon dreams wrecked and hopes broken. Many who read these words have traveled very unexpected paths during the year which dies this week, and possibly some find it hard to think of anything now except the great blow which has made the year one of crisis in their earthly history. Loss of sight, loss of hearing, loss of property, loss of health, loss of companionship, loss of a dear one who made life a beautiful and happy thing—such an experience, as any one of these, changes the world through and through for us, and such a calamity seems to inflict a permanent defeat. It seems to force upon us the feeling that we are in a stubborn world which does not care much for our wishes, or our hopes, or our ideals. Some great stunning blow smites through our best armor and spoils all the plans which we have made. What shall we say?

This: No world would be a good world to live in if everything came to us just as we wanted it. We should be weak, spoiled children—not true, noble sons of God. We must learn to shape our lives in a world which presents difficulties and trials. We must seek to get a spirit within us which overcomes the world and triumphs in spite of the hard thing which lies across the track. The greatest service which Christ's religion renders us on earth is the power which it gives us to turn these seeming defeats into triumphal chariots.

"I wanted my property and the life of comfort and ease which it could give—an unexpected occurrence has taken it from me," some one may say. Very well. The next thing for you to do is to show that you can rise above this accident of property and manifest a patient, courageous disposition in an honest struggle with poverty. The world needs a *poor saint* much more than it needs one more person living in comfort and ease. Come, then, and be that poor saint! and learn a beatitude you would never have fathomed if your purse string had not broken!

Or another will say, "It is so hard to sit

quietly still, useless and helpless, while I could do so much if I only had the health and strength." Yes, dear friend, that is hard. It is a bitter trial. But what a beautiful chariot may be made out of that trial! There are few ministries as great as the ministry of exhibiting to a household the power of Christ to make you sweet and patient and thoughtful and loving. There are plenty of persons who can preach and write books and do the world's work. This actual *practice* of the love and patience of God in the little narrow circle is more convincing than a whole city full of formal churches. And just now God wants you to do that.

Ah, but that other loss—how shall we dare touch upon it? That severing of companionship, that breaking of ties, that separation which leaves the world so empty—how shall one face *that,* and turn it into a chariot? This is sacred ground; the shoes must come off and the head be uncovered. But there is a word which must be spoken. Even here Christ gives power to *overcome* and to lead captivity captive. "I must now turn my private grief into public service," were the noble words of a man who had just experienced an unspeakably hard loss. This is the true attitude; this is the spirit of Christian faith. Grieve we must, and suffer we certainly shall if we love, but the truer the love the more it will enable us to rise above the earthly loss which seems to defeat it and to prove that it inspires us still, though the special object of our love has vanished. The greatest service of the loved object is that it trains and prepares us for wider, more universal love. He loves best who makes his private love nourish and quicken a love which reaches beyond these narrow limitations.

> " God gives us love. Something to love
>   He lends us; but when love is grown
> To ripeness, that on which it throve
>   Falls off, and love is left alone."

CHAPTER LVII

THE MINISTRY OF ORDINARY PEOPLE

IT is all very well to preach a great moving sermon for people to talk about after it is done, but there are a great many other ways of sowing the seeds of the kingdom which may do just as much good. We are apt to say, after listening to the great sermon, "Yes, it was great, but then he has preached so much and had so many opportunities that he ought to be able to speak like that. Anybody can do a thing well which he is doing all the time!" It is a fact, is it not? that few persons are really brought to a change of life by listening to what are usually called great sermons.

Most of us remember that the thing which affected our lives most, and really changed our hearts, was some personal word spoken directly to us, some close appeal which we could not shake off. We do not discover our need or cry out for mercy while we are listening to the fine discourse or the solid logic of some trained preacher. The tears are much more apt to well up, and the heart to soften under some broken testimony of a brother or sister like ourselves. Few things count for so much as the simple word spoken by the roadside, or at a casual meeting—the word which comes all fresh and unstudied from a tender, loving heart that has had its great experience.

A sinner can stand almost any amount of public preaching and go on his way unchanged, but he can seldom rise the same man from a close, intimate, face to face talk about the issues of life. It is more convincing when a person just like ourselves comes to speak to us. We know it is done for nothing else than for love's sake, and it is hard to resist such an attack upon our inner fortress.

The best Christian ministry is that done by the "unordained" persons, who have, however, had "the mighty ordination of the piercèd hands." To go quietly about one's ordinary tasks and callings, and to use the little daily chances for witnessing to the power of the Saviour is to do the best sort of ministering. It makes one happy to know that all about us, with no official robes upon them and no tiaras on their heads, there are many of these ordinary saints who are unaware that their faces shine.

CHAPTER LVIII

IT WORKS

THIS is one of Paul's great words—It WORKS. Any interested reader can, in a few minutes, look up the passages in which the apostle describes how his religion *works*. Here are some of his glowing expressions: "Grace worketh;" "Faith worketh;" "Love worketh;" "Hope worketh;" "the Holy Spirit worketh;" "a new creation" worketh, i. e., *avails;* "Tribulation worketh;" "this light affliction worketh;" "Godly sorrow worketh;" "All things *work* for those that love God"! What a religion of practical power that is! How it fits the time!

"Will it work?" is the first question which everybody in these busy days asks of everything which claims attention. Some man suggests tapping Niagara and using a little side stream to generate electrical power. Will it work? is the eager question. As soon as it is well proved that it does work, there is a rush of capital for investment in Niagara power. When the news came that it was possible to telegraph without wires, most persons doubted. It must be a wild imagination. But no, a single word is clicked across the ocean, and soon all the great steamers go out equipped with apparatus and keep up intercourse from shore to shore. *It works.* Everybody believes in it now.

Why is it so hard to raise money for constructing airships? Why do we take so little interest in the stories about them? They are deadly machines so far. They fail to work. Attempts to extract gold out of sea water, and to make diamonds out of charcoal have from time to time been made, but these undertakings do not *work*. There *is* gold in sea water, and charcoal and diamonds are both composed of carbon, but we lack a working process. Stock in "gold-from-sea-water" companies is absolutely worthless. Telephone stock is good, because the telephone works.

Sooner or later the world comes back from bogus religions to one which *works*. Human nature loves to experiment, and every new fashion, even in religions, gets tried, for its hour. But the deep heart of man in the time of stress and strain, when the reins are tested, wants a religion that *works*. A thousand forms of religion have died out of memory and are as weak to-day as the beams of Noah's ark. But the great life-currents of Christ's religion flow on for the healing both of men and of nations. It still works. It works wherever it is fairly tried. Darwin was amazed when he saw what Christianity was doing for the Tahiti savages. He wrote: "The lesson of the missionaries is the enchanter's wand; the march of improvement consequent on the introduction of Christianity in the South Seas probably stands by itself in the records of history." No; it does not stand alone. The similar record comes from all peoples where the same gospel is tried. It made over the bloody German warriors into Christian men, and it has the same power to-day, whether it is tried in Palestine, in New York slums or in the home of the city millionaire. Wherever it gets a chance it *works*. The truth is as new as to-day and as old as the Apostle James that a faith that does not *work* is dead. There is little hope for a religion of which it cannot be said, *it worketh*.

CHAPTER LIX

UNDER THE JUNIPER TREE

"WHAT doest thou here, Elijah?" was the word which came to the prophet, sitting discouraged under the juniper tree. The prophet had a hard proposition to face. His people were drifting away from their faith. Destructive forces were at work wherever he looked. He himself seemed to be alone in the battle against the incoming corrupt "religion." He took the bad course, which we are all so apt to take. He sat down and counted up the difficulties—took account of his liabilities, as the business man would say. "There is that wicked Jezebel intrenched in the land. Everybody is afraid of her. Her priests have frightened away the priests of the Lord. All the power of the kingdom is on her side. I am all alone, and I am the last prop left to the cause of Jehovah, my God!"

But the most discouraging thing, after all, for the prophet is that God is doing nothing to save His cause. He has forces enough. Why doesn't He use them to destroy these enemies of His? There is His whirlwind, which tears up the mightiest tree as though it were a straw, and which even rends mountains. Mightier still for destruction is the earthquake, which cleaves open the solid earth, and which might be used to swallow up this whole host of idol-worshipers. Most dreadful of all God's forces is the fire of the sky—the lightning. How easy it would be to cleanse the whole earth of these corrupters with such forces as these, but God does not use one of them for this purpose. God does not come in wind, in earthquake or in fire.

"What art thou doing, Elijah?" Nothing. His despondency came from thinking of the difficulties and from wondering why God did not perform some overwhelming miracle. The best cure for such despondency is to get up and get to work. The man who goes to work in the line of his duty finds that the God who did not come in the great forces of nature—wind, earthquake, fire—does come in quieter, and in less striking ways, as the power which makes use of a feeble human instrument.

"What art thou doing?" is God's word to every despondent person to-day who is moaning over the dark outlook and the great castles of difficulty which lie there in front. This is the only cure for despair and pessimism and despondency—to do the next thing which needs doing straight before one's face. The doers of deeds are always hopeful and cheerful. Those who are girding themselves to do out their clear, plain duties, however petty and small they may seem, always see the sky reddening for a new dawn. The other lesson which Elijah learned is one for us, too, to learn, that, instead of using giant forces of nature in His spiritual work, God uses and must use human hands and feet and voices. His work is done by such slight things as us. He does not send irresistible forces to destroy sinners. He sends consecrated men and women to work among them and to bring the silent forces of light and truth and love and the divine Spirit to work upon them, until, lo! they are changed. Victories are not won under juniper trees, but rather by doing what needs to be done.

CHAPTER LX

BECOMING LIKE LITTLE CHILDREN

AMONG the conditions of entrance to the kingdom of heaven which Christ lays down is this: "Except ye be converted and become as little children ye shall not enter the kingdom of heaven." Now, to understand this saying, one must understand the three stages in the life of a person. The first stage is one of unconsciousness, of absolute dependence on others for everything which furthers life. We are *made* dependent. We are taken care of. Our very bodies are formed in such a way that they adjust themselves to the environment without any conscious direction. A bright light makes the lid close to guard the eye. The presence of the source of food makes the lips do their part toward feeding the tiny body. Intricate and complicated actions are performed with no more idea of an end in view than the locomotive has when it starts for Pittsburg. All the earliest operations and acquisitions are learned by blind obedience to external stimulus. The child simply submits to the great forces which work upon him, and this implicit submission constructs his life. His whole part in the drama of life at this stage is to let the powers outside himself have their way with him unhindered.

But each seemingly blind action awakens consciousness just a little. Every movement, however instinctive, produces a slight contribution to the little fellow's sense of his own power. He rapidly begins to get a *will* of his own, and conscious purposes appear. He resists on occasion now, and asserts himself against the combined powers of the world. In very loud tones he reads off his declaration of independence. He is no longer unconscious and blindly obedient. He has discovered himself and has decided to be some sort of an independent person. The things he learns now he learns by conscious effort. He thinks of himself in all he does. He must watch his hands whenever he is gaining any new skill. He is slow and bungling. His constant foe is self-consciousness. He does nothing very well because he can never lose himself.

But there comes a new and higher stage. Actions which had been performed by slow and painful effort become natural and easy. The stroke, the touch, the act becomes sure, graceful, skillful. It no longer requires direct control of will or guard of thought. The actor now forgets himself. He does the right thing the right way without thinking. Consciousness sets the goal or end, and then sub-conscious powers, trained to do it, take up the action and carry it through with almost perfect precision. We have passed from unconsciousness, through self-consciousness, to a new and remarkable kind of unconsciousness. The person at this final stage corresponds with his environment with the same accuracy and precision which marked the blind instinct of the child, but this has been gained by a process of effort which has mastered the self and turned it over, no longer blind, but still obedient, to the great demands of the universe upon it.

But what has all this to do with the kingdom of God? Just this: A man must get not only beyond that first stage of blind instinct, but also beyond the second stage in which goodness is the result of hard and painful effort. Good deeds are all spoiled and bungled at this stage because the trail of the self lies over them all, and if one does not hold himself by sheer effort to his duty, he may slide off any minute into some path of natural instinct. Now we see that *"becoming like* a little child" is very different from *"being* a little child." It is life in our third stage, in which the action has become natural and unconscious, but only because the powers of the person have been mastered by conscious effort and *made* responsive, by an act of the will, to the calls that are made upon them. The goodness Christ seeks is no calculating goodness, no goodness through which you can hear all the machinery of the self creak. It is a goodness which has been formed by conscious obedience to Him until it becomes this self-forgetful, spontaneous goodness which bursts forth by a kind of second nature, and is as unstudied and as unconscious of results to self as the child's instinct. Acts and deeds of love now sprout out and flourish as naturally as once the selfish ones did. Such a man doing the good deed is almost surprised to hear it praised. His only answer is, "How otherwise?"

CHAPTER LXI

THE MOST SERIOUS SCEPTICISM

THE Hebrew prophet saw God everywhere in the actual life and work of men. The people about him believed in God for religious purposes. He was for them a being who was flattered by prayer and pleased with the smell of incense. He troubled Himself very little, they thought, with the affairs of men, so long as they "did their religion" on Sabbath days and at appointed times. There was a complete break between "religion" and daily life. On week-days a man could "devour widows' houses," and on the holy day the same man could piously pray through his "long prayer." The prophets called this pretense by its right name. It was empty, hollow sham. It was sheer irreligion. They proclaimed a God who is concerned in the affairs of actual life; who is at the heart of justice and mercy; who is present wherever righteousness and goodness appear; who not only rides on the wings of the wind, but who moves unseen wherever the moral forces of the world are arrayed. He is an actual power in the personal life, in the home life, in the community life, in the civic and national life. His eyes run to and fro through all the earth. He holds the plumbline in His hand and tests everything by it. He winnows men as the farmer winnows his grain. He knows the inward man and cares not for the vain oblation and the hollow tramp of the Temple.

The prophets had a single standard for all life—whether in the Temple or in the market. The people had a double standard. They believed in God and served Him when they were using the religious standard. They disregarded Him and disbelieved in Him the rest of the time. The result was that they turned out to be thorough sceptics. They did not believe in any real God who lived in the lives of men and who was concerned in the affairs of the world. Their God was a poor, weak Sovereign who held His court only on holy days, and who either slept or was on a journey the rest of the time. He could be ignored except on occasions when "worship" was in order.

This is the prevailing scepticism of our time. Honest intellectual doubt and questioning are easily cured. All the doubter needs is to see a little deeper, to go below the surface and find the truth he is earnestly seeking. That other scepticism is dreadfully serious. It eats the life out of a man before he knows it. It saps his inward strength and leaves him a hollow shell while he half believes he has a religion. The disease of this scepticism is eating at the heart of any man who doubts whether it is worth while to keep his soul pure and stainless. It is sapping any man who attempts to practise the double standard. It is working havoc in all men who conclude that religion cannot be put into daily life. To make God a toy for the altar, a being who cares for nothing but prayers and incense, is to give Him up altogether. It is to settle down into a real scepticism unspeakably more dangerous than that of the man who honestly questions because he is determined to find the true God. This double standard scepticism is very common and very ominous. It is not cured in a day nor by easy methods. It calls for the patient, faithful work of a line of true prophets who can again proclaim the living God, and, better still, it calls for a generation of men and women who by their quiet, solid, transparent lives shall *compel* men to see the fruit of faith in our God.

CHAPTER LXII

WHAT NOT TO PRAY FOR

PROBABLY every serious Christian has often felt his poverty of spirit as he bows before his Father in prayer. It is a sublime spectacle—a finite, needy mortal face to face with God, talking with Him. It is the highest activity of the soul. But what shall I say when I come before this Infinite Being? What shall I tell Him? What shall I ask for? There is nothing which so tests the spiritual quality of one's life. A person can get on pretty well with small spiritual attainments, so long as he only exhorts or testifies or preaches or gives addresses. But as soon as he begins to talk with God, we discover whether he is rich or poor in the things of the spirit. We shall now spy out the nakedness of his inward life if it exists, or we shall see the wideness of his spiritual reach. No easy flow of words, no glibness of tongue, will do here. The man who is really spiritual will show that he is acquainted with God, that he is at home in His presence. Doubtless we have all felt, as the great apostle did, that we hardly know what to pray for as we ought. It is only as a person enters more deeply into the life of the Spirit that he sees the true things to ask for, so that the increase in the power of prayer is a good test of spiritual growth. But are there not some things which we all ought to avoid praying for? First of all, of course, we ought to rise above selfish desires when we come before God. He who looks upon prayer as a means to the gratification of selfish desires—he who looks upon prayer as a short road to success— will never rise very high in the spiritual life. God becomes to him a means to some little narrow end of his own instead of being Himself the all-sufficing object of love and aspiration. This is too much like the poor idol-worshiper who beats his god when He fails to give him what he asks for!

We ought not to use prayer as a method of relieving us from our own duties and from a proper effort. No one should allow his prayers for the poor and the suffering to excuse him from his own responsibility toward them. He is, too, a poor citizen who prays for his country on election day and then goes off fishing or casts a thoughtless ballot for candidates who are pledged to the very opposite of what he prayed for!

Finally, we ought not to pray for things which dishonor God. Just here many of us fail. How often we hear the words, "O Lord, be kind and loving to us," or, "O Lord, meet with us to-day," or "Come into our hearts," or "Send thy spirit," and a whole series of expressions which imply that God is capricious or far-away or unloving. Such words show an ignorance of the revelation of God in Christ. To ask God to be loving is like asking that lead should be heavy! It is His nature to be loving. He always is. An earthly child who kept asking his human father to be good and kind and loving would be dishonoring his father— such words would grieve a father. Have I been so long time with you and you do not yet know My love? Then again there can be no need to ask God to come; to send His Spirit. Wherever any meet in His name He *is* there. Wherever any heart is open to the entrance of the Spirit He *is there*. We would never ask that the sunlight might be sent into our houses. It is the nature of sunlight to come in. The only thing which keeps it out is the closing of blinds and shutters. Fling them open and in it comes. So too God. He never stays out of a soul that makes place for Him. To beg Him to be true to His own nature is to dishonor Him. It either means that we are ignorant of

His nature, or that we are afraid to trust Him. The real trouble often is that we pray without thinking of what our words imply—we are not putting our real meaning into our words. Such praying will not help us grow spiritually, for mere lip praying may easily become an empty form. The lesson we all need most to learn is how to make our prayers always voice the sincere purpose of our *hearts*.

CHAPTER LXIII.

THE PRACTICE OF THE LOVE OF GOD.

THERE is one thing which even the simplest Christian of us may learn from the scientist. He will never be satisfied with any theory or hypothesis until he has tried it. He goes straight to work to see if it can stand the strain and test of facts. Every page in the history of science is strewn with rejected theories and dead hypotheses. The laws and principles which are taught to-day are held because they have survived the hardest test of actual facts which so far are known. Everything in the world gains in value as it proves able to stand tests. This is especially true of the great things by which we live. There is a whole world of difference between second-hand accounts of somebody else's experience and first-hand experience itself. We begin, of course, with truths which others have tested and which we accept on authority, but we never quite *possess* our truth until we have worked it out in practice and put it to the strain of living by it. Little by little we pass over from mere views and opinions which have been given to us to the deeper, solider faith which is the fruit and product of the actual practice of our principles and doctrines. Christianity first begins to be something mighty when a person is found who goes beyond views and theories and really practises in his life the great truths which lie at its heart.

Every Christian creed which has held its place in the world has announced in one way or another the Fatherhood and Love of God as a central fact. For ages men have said, "I believe in God the Father," but too often they have gone on living as though this belief made no difference to them. It never seemed to occur to them that they had to *practise* it—*i. e.*, that they ought to live as though they knew God as a Father. We all find it easy to say over John's great words, "God is Love," but we are very slow in practising this truth until it has all the reality of the things which we touch and see. Think what it means! Let us start out to translate all our creed, all our doctrines into actual practice. We will live to-day, this week, this month, this year as though we knew that our life solidly rested on the love of God. It is to be as sure a fact for us as space or gravitation. Wherever we move we are enveloped in it. Well, the effect would be, first of all, to wipe out completely our anxiety and our worry. We worry because we lack confidence in the future, but the man who lives in the love of God knows that He who clothes the lily and guides the bird is shaping his life toward good ends even when he cannot see the way, and so he trusts and is happy. He stops being burdened with himself because this very practice of the love of God makes him care more for others than for himself, and he forgets his own troubles in his joy to help ease somebody else's trouble. Furthermore, if we actually realized what the love of God means and lived as though we knew its meaning, we should stop sinning. We sin because we want something for our own selves. We are blind to what our sin will make God suffer. We forget that the mightiest thing in the universe is the love of God, and we blur the cost of His sacrifice for us in our desire to get some petty thing for ourselves. The moment we feel the tug of His love upon us and go to living with a sense of the fact that every sin in the world crucifies Him afresh and spoils His purpose for us and in us sin becomes a hideous thing, and His infinite love constrains us to live not unto ourselves, but unto Him.

Then, too, he who truly practises the love of God can face the mysteries which look so dark from the outside. "I am not afraid," said the little fellow at sea in the storm, "because my father is the captain." That is the secret of all triumph in this world of trial and loss—"I know my Father is pilot on this sea of life, even though the mists are thick." There can be no shipwreck for the soul that practises that faith. To live in the love of God is to win eternally everything which is lost in time and space. He who loves us to the death cannot bring into our lives anything which defeats or breaks our human loves. That is impossible. His whole purpose is to perfect and heighten our love, never to crush or weaken it. As we live in the confidence of His love and practise it we shall rise above the faith which is only belief and opinion to the faith which is the very substance of the things we hope for, the test of things not seen.

CHAPTER LXIV.

HAS CHRISTIANITY BEEN TRIED?

THE remark is sometimes made that Christianity has failed. On the contrary, it has not yet been fairly tried. Wherever it has really been tried it has proved to be a transforming force of the highest order. "Give me five hundred men," cried Phillips Brooks; "nay, give me one hundred men of the spirit that I know to-day in *three men,* and I will answer for it that the city shall be saved." Yes, so would we all answer for it, if we could get the hundred men. But Christianity means, or ought to mean, new men of this sort, the Spirit of Christ reproduced in men's lives. That is just what apostolic Christianity was, and does anybody think *that* was a failure? Why is it, then, that we look in vain for our hundred men who shall save the city? Because so few of us realize at all that we are expected to re-live and reproduce Christ's life in the world. Paul knew it, and John knew it, and they did it; and wherever they went there were dynamic results.

But little by little Christianity became something else, something quite different. The religion of personal spiritual life, lived in the power of the resurrected Christ, was changed into an Institution, with elaborate machinery for dispensing everything essential to man's salvation. Conformity to the Institution took the place of obedience to the living Lord. The simple, living faith in a personal Christ was changed into a system of thought, a body of intellectual views, to be "held" as a creed. Priestly mediation took the place of the free intercourse of the soul with the loving, forgiving Father whom Christ had revealed at such infinite cost. This seemed a much easier religion than the original apostolic type because it was not difficult to stand fairly well and yet be only a "nominal" Christian, *i. e.*, a Christian in name. The bad habit grew, and alas, came right over into Protestantism. For lo, these hundreds of years Christians have been trying to settle a lot of questions which have no more bearing on real, essential Christianity than the question whether Mars is inhabited has. These questions have steadily kept Christianity running off on side tracks, and, worst of all, have continually produced dissension and bad blood.

Meantime, the world is losing all interest in these quarrels and dissensions. They help nobody, they comfort nobody, they save nobody.

"The hungry sheep look up and are not fed."
That sort of thing *has failed*. It does no good
work in the world. Its knell is struck. But
that does not mean that Christianity has failed.
We are learning that the real question is, "Am
I manifesting Christ"? We are coming back
to the early basis of Christianity, which was
faith in Christ, and obedience to Him. As soon
as a man appears who has the Spirit of Christ,
and whose life reflects the divine goodness and
love, he does what the apostolic men did—he
moves and influences and transforms men.
Those who live in the power of God shake the
world as of old. The thing most needed now is
just a genuine trial of real Christianity, which
means HUMAN LIVES TRANSFORMED BY CHRIST
AND FILLED WITH GOD. Our cities, our rural
districts, aye, our nation itself can still be saved
if we could get a living nucleus of such lives.
Thou, dear Friend, who readest this, may be
one of the hundred in thy community.

CHAPTER LXV.

BEAUTY IN RELIGION

THOSE who have charge of the education of children have discovered that nothing exercises such a moulding influence over the little lives as beautiful surroundings and beautiful objects. The child who has formed a deep love for *beautiful* things is well on his way toward a love for *good* things. Children instinctively feel the power of a beautiful face. Roses on the desk, bright paper on the walls, attractive pictures, growing plants in the windows—all these things play their part in making children good. Music reaches the hidden life in a child in a way that nothing else does. Harmony belongs to the very inner nature of things, and it certainly exercises a subtle power in the ordering of the life in its early formative period. The importance of beauty in early training lies in the fact that it reaches deeper than consciousness and affects the disposition and underlying nature itself. What is learned may be forgotten; what is silently wrought into the sub-conscious self will not fade out with time.

What has all this to do with religion? Very much, indeed. The influence of beauty in religion is often enough overlooked, but it is nevertheless a decidedly important fact. The pleading of a beautiful voice is instantly felt even by the roughest people. Hearts respond at once when the "beauty of holiness" appears in a life which is before them. There is always a deep power over a meeting when the praise is felt to be "comely," *i. e.,* beautiful. A more restful sense steals upon any worshiper when the room in which he sits is harmonious and attractive than when it is cheerless and barnlike. The soul demands beauty, and therefore the rough and ugly can never help on the true religious life. God must love beauty, or He would not have filled the earth and heavens with it, and it is the almost universal experience that when we feel deeply moved by beauty God always seems near.

It is not possible for most of us to meet in buildings which are beautiful in their architecture; where the arches are groined in perfect curves, where the pillars completely express the laws of symmetry. We have plain houses, built often by the hands of our own members. This is all very well. But the room where we gather should be as comely and as fitting as our tastes and abilities will permit. It should be as beautiful as it can be. It should have the freshest, sweetest air there is in the world, and the needs of the little ones should not be forgotten. But most important of all, the meeting itself must have the spirit of beauty in it. Athletic prizes to-day are not given to the performers who do wonderful feats, but to those who perform their feats with grace and beauty. Let us catch a hint from the athlete. Let all things be fitting. The *manner* in which one prays counts tremendously. Earthly courts are weighed down with etiquette, but it is well to come before our heavenly King with a manner which befits His majesty. The effect of a beautiful prayer is something indescribable. The same thing is true with the message of the gospel. Some of us are too old to change our tones or our manners. But let the young speaker learn early that what he says will count much more if it is seasoned with the salt of grace. Not only the "feet," but the whole bearing, "of those who bring good tidings," should be beautiful. How we all might profit by obeying Paul's word: "Whatsoever things are true, honorable, just, pure, *lovely,* of good report, virtuous and praiseworthy, set your thoughts on these" (Phil. 4: 8).

CHAPTER LXVI

THE LIFE OF LIBERTY

NOBODY begins with liberty. It would be ruinous to say to the child: "Do just what you like to." Quite the opposite course is followed by the loving parent. He teaches the child the meaning of "thou must" and "thou shalt." The boy thus learns to obey, to adjust himself to the will of others. He discovers that his field of freedom is very narrow indeed. When he gets to school he is obliged to learn the limits of his freedom in a new way. He cannot accept as truth anything that happens to strike his fancy. He must find out what really is true and accept that. He must get his set lesson. He must learn what the book says. He must remember what the teacher tells him, whether he likes the facts which are presented or not, he must master them; and if his lesson is not learned, he must stay after school and get it. In society again nobody is quite free. There are laws and customs and institutions which force our lives in certain directions. The man who is not good by nature (and who is?) must be taught by law to observe the rights and privileges of others. Society never trusts men to realize their lives according to their own sweet will. Back of the law there is force. You disobey at your peril. Even in religion there are the stages of fear and of commandments. Primitive religion is largely grounded in fear. The worshiper brings his sacrifice because he is afraid of God and hopes to appease Him. He crawls on his hands and knees and inflicts frightful bodily torture because he believes it will keep his god from punishing him in a worse way. In the next stage he obeys the law or the commandment because he thinks this will win God's favor; he scrupulously fulfills His ordinances, His ceremonies or His ritual because he expects a great return from the God whom he has thus served.

But it is our privilege, nay, more, our high calling, to pass over from this life of restraint, of fear, of law to a life of glorious liberty, of joyous freedom. The child who has been drilled into obedience has little by little discovered the spirit of love in the discipline, the goodness of those who have restrained him. Now he begins to be good, not because he must, but because he chooses to be good. He has lost the incentive of fear, and has gained the incentive of love. As a result you have the wonderful spectacle of the son resigning his own dreams and prospects in order to support the family he loves, the daughter giving up every ambition to be the stay and comfort of a father in his declining years, or of a mother who needs her—and doing it, too, from free and glad choice. So, too, the scholar passes from the tasks that are *set,* to become an independent searcher after truth, making his own free contribution in the chosen field of his research. The citizen almost forgets that there are laws to be obeyed. Instead of needing restraint, he devotes himself to the task of righting the wrongs, of destroying corruption, of purifying the State. Through his love for his country and for man he contributes all his powers for the puropse of helping other men attain a wider freedom and a richer life.

Do we not also pass over from religion of fear and religion of external commandments to a religion of joyous liberty and devoted love—where our only law is the law of the spirit of life in Christ Jesus? The entire work of our Lord is directed to carry us over to this freedom of fullgrown sons. His method is to kindle in us incentives of love and devotion. He reveals the Divine love and yearning. He appeals to us through His own sacrifice to save us. "Thou needs must love me who have died for thee." He shows us the unlimited possibilities of life. "You can be like your heavenly Father." There is no force, no compulsion, no rigid external system to fit into. We are called to the freedom of sons. We are pointed away to the ever-widening goal of a perfect life. The types of the blessed life which He gives us are those who hunger for more righteousness, those who feel the poverty of their spirits, and so are open to the light and receptive of the truth, those who are purifying their hearts so that God is continually growing clearer to their vision. Those who thus feel the compulsion of love have entered the life of liberty. They do right now, not because they must, but because the joy of their lives is in doing right. The law is not left behind, but it is swallowed up in the free will to choose the life of moral action. "I delight to do thy will" is the psalmist's word for this attainment. "So speak and so do," says James, "as they that shall be judged, by the law of liberty." What a day of judgment! How many of us can God trust to such absolute freedom— no law but our own free will!

www.ingramcontent.com/pod-product-compliance
Lightning Source LLC
Chambersburg PA
CBHW070247230426
43664CB00014B/2433